WEV

DOPE

THE STONED & STUPID MISADVENTURES OF A WALLY NAMED WEV

A MEMOIR. SORT OF.
VOLUME 1

DISCLAIMER

The events depicted in this book actually fucking happened.
They have not been fictionalised or embellished. All the names,
some locations and some story details, have been changed to
protect identities. Even the Author can barely work out who's
who anymore, so good luck trying.

ABOUT THE
AUTHOR

For most of his young adult life, Wev was a drug addict and an alcoholic. He spent those days roaming East London, consuming fun in all shapes and sizes, including heroin, cocaine, weed, speed, and, worst of all, cans of warm Foster's. With his gang of best mates by his side, Wev squeezed the life out of the proverbial lemon so much it turned into a diamond.

As Wev grew older in age (but not maturity), he moved from London to Hong Kong (and back again) with his adult job, in between travelling the world with his friends, finding mayhem, misadventure and madness everywhere they went, and often packing it in their bags, just to ensure a good time wasn't far behind.

In his forties, Wev finally found a home in the Middle East, where he now lives with his wife, two children and two cats. This is his first book.

DOPEWEV.COM

CONTENTS

Wev-on-Sea, Brighton

I'M WITH STUPID

I've done a lot of stupid shit in my life. I mean, *really* stupid shit. The kind of stuff, as you'll soon learn, that borders on probable insanity.

I should be dead. I should be in jail. I should be in an asylum. And that's not a humble-brag, that's an admission of guilt. I should have learned *some* lessons.

I didn't.

So, here we are. I'm an idiot, and proud, and I am responsible for all of it. But – let's not forget – it's a dumb fucking world full of idiots even worse than me, so I'm just a victim of the system, right? I'm sure you're no better. I'm sure you've done stuff that is incredibly silly too. The type of stuff you look back at and wonder, *"How am I still alive?"*

The only difference between you and me is … I'm stupid enough to write a book incriminating myself.

Obviously, some of the ridiculous nonsense I have done over the past 30 years (and counting) was under the heaving influence of the best/worst drugs known to humanity, some under the emotional duress of alcohol. The rest, I'm proud to admit, was all down to me and my natural sense of curiosity with the world in which we all live; me, in search of the ridiculousness present in most situations, pushing boundaries. If stupidity was a bear in a cage, I would want to poke it. While in the cage with it. Even today, I regularly approach strangers and greet them with a big cheesy grin and a hearty hello, just for that human interaction, to see where it may take me. If any old fucker (or animal) approaches me and starts gibbering, I will always take the time to listen to what they have to say, no matter how mental I may appear. I'm old school.

I don't take life seriously and will always find time to laugh in any situation, no matter how serious or inappropriate. We only get a short amount of time on this planet, so we might as well say "Yes!" to everything and then laugh about it the next day (if you're still alive). You might as well just smile, deal with it and go in search of things that will make you laugh. I am a far happier person – and better husband and father – for doing so. My search for silliness – it usually finds me, just FYI – has often put me in awkward situations. But I embrace awkwardness. I embrace ridicule. I embrace the stupidity of life around me. I am happy being Wev and I don't care at all what other people think of me. I've embraced who I am, achieved more than I could ever have imagined and had way too much fun along the way. And I want my life – my misadventures – to inspire you in the same way, without getting all pretentious about it.

Monkey see. Monkey do.

Unfortunately, due to the aforementioned drugs and alcohol, a lot of the most insane shit that I have done has largely been forgotten. Thankfully, a lot has been retained in my somewhat tainted unconsciousness and in the memories of my friends. During the 2020 lockdown, with little else to do except be a parent, I felt that this was the right time to write it all down before I lose it all forever.

Look at the world around you. Look at the presidents and prime ministers that are and have been running the countries recently. Idiots. Look at how the world reacts to lockdown and the COVID-19 pandemic. Chaos. Look at the political correctness gone crazy. Mental. Look at social media where everybody is now too conscious of how they look and appear to the wider world – afraid of falling victim to so-called cancel culture – that they are too scared to let their hair down and just friggin' enjoy themselves. There's something in the air right now. Stupidity seems to prevail at a level much higher than you. So, if you can't beat them – join them. Right?

It's a fucked-up world out there, run by a bunch of stupid cunts. You know this to be true. I believe the generation I grew up in, the 1980s, was the last generation when you could just go out, do what you wanted, have a good time, get loaded, and not care what other people thought. I want the readers of this book to remember that before the internet and iPhones, there was a time when life existed outside the borders of a black mirror. And, most importantly, I want to prove to the world that no matter how crazy, or dumb, life is around them, that it is possible to live, thrive and survive stupidity, no matter its shape or size.

How do I know? Because that is exactly what I have done.

I am living proof that being stupid is the best thing since, well, stupidity came sliced...

looking for drugs, probably

I AM WEV

Hello. My name is Wev. Except it isn't. Not really. But you knew that. I'm stupid. But not *that* stupid. "Wev" – me – was born in Liverpool, 1973. I moved down to East London just as my basic grasp of language started to form. This move gave me the distinct honour of being the only Scouser alive with a Boycie accent. You know, the caricature from *Only Fools and Horses*.

I have two sisters called Woo (older) and Moo (younger). I mention them a bit. We grew up on a council estate in Dartford with my parents, Lin and Dave (LAD whenever referenced as a collective). At primary school, I was a bit of a golden boy and managed to wangle my way into Dartford Grammar School (same one Mick Jagger attended, FYI). Naturally, I lost all my childhood friends when I went there, as they all went to the local comprehensive and thought that I was some sort of posh cunt for going to the grammar. Remember, this was the eighties. Kids were cruel. This led to me having to take detours through the back streets and alleyways on my way home from school, so that I could avoid being beaten the shit out of by the local comprehensive kids for being a "grammar school cunt".

I never really fitted in at that school, as most of the students were from the rich villages that surround Dartford. There were only about five of us from my town that studied there and each of us were on the periphery of popularity, due to us being from poor backgrounds. I always remember the teachers trying to drill into us that we were the top three per cent and that we should live our lives with that imprinted in our minds. Even then, I always wondered, "The top 3 per cent of what? Of being self-serving, elitist fuckers?"

It wasn't long before I fell into the local drug scene. Must have been when I was about 15. Despite being labelled a smart kid, I fucked up my GCSE's due to being stoned during the exams. I achieved seven C-level grades and one D-level grade. This was a long way away from a top-three-per-cent performance.

As soon as I could, and to fund my burgeoning booze and drug habit, I started working. I found local jobs stacking shelves in nearby corner shops, at a hospital kitchen and at a fruit and veg shop. Pretty soon, I was making quite a bit of bank. The money was spent on hip-hop vinyl records and drugs. I started selling acid and weed, which obviously brought the trappings of more money than you could dream of earning legally as a 16-year-old turd. It wasn't long before I had friendships with the very same people that bullied me throughout my school days. Obviously, not being one to hold grudges, I mixed any weed I sold them, with a healthy dosage of catnip from the local pet shop.

As my drug intake increased, I realised I needed to find a proper job, with proper earnings. I found a temporary placement (that turned into a permanent job) in the City of London with one of the largest property agents in the UK. I stayed there for six years, progressing to Management Accountant level. The advancement of my career coincided with the progression of my love of drugs. Ganja – as I call it; yes, I'm old – remained a constant. But soon the acid turned into mushrooms, which elevated to glue, then speed, then ecstasy and, of course, cocaine. Yes, what a cliché. Weed, for me, was the gateway drug. To Heaven.

Music was a gateway too. My tastes moved on from hip-hop to seventies rock and pop – Cat Stevens, early Genesis, Led Zeppelin, Jethro Tull, Hendrix, the Doors, Black Sabbath and Hawkwind, in particular. I also fell in love with African music (due to Peter Gabriel starting up the Real World Record label) and reggae music, which was an extension of the ragamuffin hip-hop sound that was emerging in the UK at the time. Festivals became a big part of my life and Glastonbury became an annual pilgrimage.

At 20, I left home and moved to Peckham with Nelson and MJ,

two friends from Dartford. The next five years were spent flitting around rat-infested squats in Peckham, Camberwell and Brixton.

In my early twenties, I left the property company and worked for a travel agent in Soho, before returning to the property company two years later, skint, and living in a shithole in Bethnal Green. Today, it's probably worth a million quid. My drug habit also now extended to crack, heroin, and ketamine.

Fun times.

At this time, a lot of my friends were "in the media", so we would frequent lots of "pretentious media bars" in Soho, selling and taking drugs with many "celebrities".

About a year later, I got sent to Hong Kong by the property company for a six-month stint that turned into seven years. I progressed from Systems Accountant to I.T. Director. I stopped taking (most) drugs but hit the booze big time. I also managed to find someone who could supply me with my beloved ganja, so carried on with that too.

While in HK, I had a mid-life crisis when I found out I had a half-brother in Liverpool, so spent a few unemployed months back in the UK to get to know him and then took one of my best friends, Dr Danger, to Venezuela for the mother of all crack binges … to wean him off heroin.

I then went back to Hong Kong and set up an agency promoting dancers and African / Latin musicians to the casinos in Macau – this did really well for a couple of years – but then I quit, as my business partner was greedy, and I couldn't handle his desire to take advantage of the people we had on our books. I quit at the wrong time, as this meant that I couldn't renew my visa, so had to move back to the UK.

I reached out to some contacts from my time as a Director and managed to get a job at an Accountancy System Vendor as a Senior Business Analyst and found a lovely pad in the centre of Greenwich. Whilst I worked there, I started up a reggae record label with my friend Chief, which was a fantastic way to spend my spare time.

Then, a phone call from a doctor informed me that I had actual brain damage, which meant that I had to quit the booze and hard drugs again. Ganja remained a big part of my life though.

I left that company when I was offered a job by a company that makes Alternative Investments Software for Sovereign Wealth Funds and Private Equity Firms (yeah – I still don't know what that means and I've been working in the industry for more than ten years). Whilst working there, I met my wife, KT, on the internet and impregnated her within three weeks of meeting her. Best stupidest move of my life. This little scenario meant that I quit the record company, moved out of Greenwich, and got a mortgage in Basingstoke (where she grew up). Basingstoke! What a stupid place to live.

One child (Bubs) became two (Squiddles). KT and I then got married. KT still moans at me about my proposal: "I've been offered a decent job far away. I suppose that means we have to get married?" She never got an engagement ring, but she did get a steady supply of me, so everything worked out.

Far away from the rest of the world, I am enjoying a standard of living I never thought possible, considering my humble working-class roots. I am proud to provide my children with an upbringing that means they would have been exactly the type of kids I would have taken an instant dislike to, as they have access to all of the things I didn't when I grew up.

I haven't lost sense of who I am and where I come from, and I ensure that my kids are well aware that they are not living a "normal" life. I have a gutter-class hatred for golf, actively avoid the expatriate crowd and even though my suits and clothes are now from designer outlets, I still manage to make them look shabby and as if they were purchased from Dartford market.

The undisclosed location where I now reside has draconian drug laws, which has meant that I now do not smoke weed. I am now officially tee-total, with a wife, two kids and two cats. Who would have thought?

I don't miss the hedonistic lifestyle I led though my tweens, teens, twenties, and thirties. I truly believe that if I hadn't lived such a full-blooded life, my life as a father and a husband would have been filled with regret and resentment. I have neither. And, I guess that's the point of this book. Being true to who I was allowed me to step away from the cliché of my roots and live a better, more evolved life, one I may never have attained if I actually listened to people telling me to "grow up". Thankfully, being the living embodiment of stupidity has kept me young at heart – even if age hasn't been kind to the rest of me.

Anyway, I hope that introduction wasn't as painful for those of you reading it, as it was for me writing it.

You know me now.

I am Wev.

Now, watch me go be stupid…

Little Wev ... and some other people

1.
HOME

When I returned back to the UK from Hong Kong around 2007, I was working as a Business Analyst for the Accountancy Software vendor referenced in the previous chapter. This meant that I spent a lot of my time travelling up and down the country, visiting academies, charities, and museums, to develop and install spanking brand-new Accountancy Systems for such establishments. It was a good gig, as I was paid a decent salary plus expenses incurred while on these site visits. This helped me fund living in a pad in the centre of Greenwich, London, and a reggae record label that didn't sell many records, as well as an expensive skunk (the drug, not the animal) habit.

I never donated money to charities because since having this job, I learned of the excessive expenditure some of these aid organisations incur by purchasing city-centre properties and snazzy office furniture, spending money on superfluous business trips around the world and paying top wages to executives rather than the poor and vulnerable. I ain't a tight old cunt, though. I give directly to people who have been less fortunate than myself. At least then I know that 100 per cent of my donation goes directly to the people who need it. Anyway, I digress…

On one such visit, I travelled up to Birmingham in the morning, and spent the day working at one of the academies in the city, where coincidentally Keels' (you'll learn of him soon enough) brother was the deputy headmaster. After work, I checked into a decent hotel. I would always bring a little bag of ganja with me on these business trips, otherwise it would have been soul-destroying. The central location of my hotel, meant I couldn't just pop outside and have a joint, due to there being a heavy footfall of pedestrians. Fortunately, the windows of my room opened, so I just stuck my head out the window and smoked my spliff. As I stood at the window, smoking, I switched on my iPod and blasted some conscious lyrics from the politically correct Sizzla Kalonji, and watched the smoke dissipate in the night sky. All was good. I couldn't be fucked to go out and eat, and I didn't want to order room service, as there was always the risk that there was a trace of weed aroma hanging around the room that would be noticeable when my food was delivered.

It was 9pm and I had just rolled my penultimate spliff of the night, when there was a knock on the door. I wondered who the fuck it could be. I shouted to whoever it was to hold on, as I put on some clothes. I tidied away the weed and Rizlas, shut the window and had a little sniff around the room. Shit. The room stunk of skunk. I edged the door open and was greeted by a middle-aged man in a suit.

"Hello. Can I help you?" I asked.

"Hello, sir. I am the manager of the hotel. I am afraid, I am going to have to ask you to leave."

"What?"

"This is a no-smoking hotel. Our policies are clear that if you smoke in your room, you will be asked to leave immediately."

"What are you talking about? I haven't been smoking in here."

"Sir. Please..."

"I don't know what you're talking about. I haven't been smoking."

"Sir, I can smell the marijuana you have been smoking from the corridor."

"Honestly, I haven't been smoking."

"We have footage from our exterior security camera of you leaning out the window – of your room – smoking."

"Really?"

"Yes. And it is clear that what you are smoking can at best be described as a very large hand-rolled cigarette."

"Ah."

"I am afraid you must leave immediately, sir. We cannot have you smoking marijuana in our hotel. If I do not report you to the police, I could get in trouble."

"Oh, come on, mon. I promise I won't smoke anymore. Can't I just stay? It's 9pm."

"Sir, you are in Birmingham city centre. There are lots of hotels. I suggest you head in the direction of New Street station and find a hotel there."

"Mate, please let me stay."

"Sir, if you do not leave within the next five minutes, I am afraid I will have to call the police."

Under my breath, I muttered, "Fucking cunt", which he most definitely heard.

With that, I shut the door of the room, packed my bag and went down to reception. The hotel manager was there, waiting for me. I handed over my key card and asked for the money I had previously paid for the night stay. He told me to poke it and leave otherwise he would call the police. I really didn't want to get arrested on a business trip for smoking weed in an expenses-paid hotel room, so cut my losses and left.

I walked down the road, towards New Street station, and came across another hotel. I entered and tried to check in. They asked for payment up front. I tried my trusty Visa Electron debit card. "Sorry, sir. I am afraid your payment has been declined."

Shit.

I was paid on the twenty-fifth of every month, and it was the night before. I knew I didn't have enough money in my bank account to pay for the room in advance, thus the declined transaction. However, I would be able to pay in the morning once my salary had cleared. I explained the situation to the receptionist and asked whether I could pay on checkout. The response from the receptionist was a big, fat, hairy, "No". I was fucked. I explained to him that I will be back once my salary had cleared my bank account and that I would see him in a couple of hours.

I left this hotel and continued my jaunt towards the train station. About 500 yards from the station, I spotted a homeless bloke sitting in a shop doorway. I had fuck all else to do, I thought, so I might as well sit down and chill out with him, while I waited for my salary to clear. I approached him and asked whether I could join him for a couple of hours. He welcomed me with loving, BO-riddled arms. He looked like he was in his mid-thirties, was obviously unwashed and unshaven, with shoulder-length hair and wearing old, dirty clothes. He sat there, leaning against the glass door of a Jigsaw with a skanky blanket wrapped around himself, using his tatty bag of shite as a pillow. I sat next to him, clean shaven, wearing an expensive Paul Smith suit, shirt, tie, and shoes combo, carrying an expensive holdall full of premium skunk. Once I got myself comfortable on the floor next to him, I pulled out my bag of ganja. He laughed.

We spent the next couple of hours gibbering shite and smoking spliff together. As with any homeless person, he had unfortunate circumstances that led him to being in the situation he was in, which in turn led to a reliance on alcohol. The homelessness made it very difficult for the poor man to get out of this situation and find any sort of stability. Begging was the only way he could make a living without a permanent address. My story of being chucked out of the hotel for smoking weed and having to wait for my hefty salary to clear paled into insignificance with what this poor man had to deal with every day.

Midnight came and went. At the nearest ATM, I checked to see whether my salary had been credited to my account. Nope.

I went back to my homeless friend and started to roll another spliff. As I sat down next to him, he extended his blanket out, and wrapped it over my shoulder. It stunk of blue cheese and was a bit crispy in parts, but it was a lovely gesture. An hour later, I decided to check my funds again. No joy. I didn't know why my salary hadn't cleared my bank yet and started contemplating that I might have to spend a night on the streets.

I returned to my friend, he looked pretty fucked. As soon as he saw me, he smiled and opened his blanket, as if to welcome me into his bosom. I gladly shuffled next to him and skinned up again. He looked at me and called me a nutter. He didn't smoke much weed, as he couldn't afford it, so this little session was properly spacing him out. I handed him the spliff, he took one puff, then handed it back to me. "Sorry mate. I can't smoke any more. I'm fucked!" I took the spliff from him and started chuffing away. Our conversation soon dried up, due to us both being tired and really stoned. After 10 minutes, I finished the spliff, stubbed it out on the floor next to me, and turned to him. He had fallen asleep, head drooped, with a little bit of dribble coming out of his mouth. I moved closer slightly and his head fell on to my shoulder.

Hours later, I was woken by the sun beaming on to my face. I was still laying in the doorway of Jigsaw, with the crusty blanket still wrapped around me. But I couldn't see my homeless mate. I then heard a shuffle and felt movement behind me.

He was fucking spooning me. For warmth, I hoped.

I sat upright, stretched, then told him that I was going to see whether I could withdraw any money. Finally, I could. I strolled back to my man, handed him £100 rent for the night and gave him the rest of my ganja, then bid him farewell. The joy on his face was greater than I've ever been able to give to any woman.

Pleased with myself, I dragged myself to the train station and found the public toilets, where I washed and brushed myself down and put a clean shirt on. I then popped into Pret-A-Manger and grabbed a couple of bananas, a croissant, and a coffee. After I ate my continental breakfast, I went to the taxi rank and was driven to the academy – who were paying £1,250 for my presence that day.

What a fucking life.

2.
DILDO GUY

While living in Hong Kong in the early noughties, as an I.T director, I was invited to the Australian branches of the property company I worked for, to install an Accounting System for them. The idea was that by sticking every region on the same accounts system and on the same chart of accounts, it would be easier for them to consolidate their finances and make reporting easier. Blah. Obviously, being a 31-year-old hedonist, I couldn't think of anything better to be doing with my life.

During one of my many stints in Sydney, I received a phone call from one of my best mates, Chief. He had just split up with the mother of his children and was in a bit of a state. I told him to get himself down to Australia for a month, to see whether that would sort his head out. He didn't have any money, so I paid for his flight and put him up in the one-bedroom serviced apartments in the Central Business District where I was staying.

Within a few days of Chief's phone call, I was hugging him at Sydney arrivals lounge, after his long journey from the UK.

It was really fun having him in Sydney. I hadn't seen him for a few months and despite the bad experience he was having with his ex-girlfriend, we were having a good laugh. Prior to Chief's arrival, I had obtained a reliable source of decent skunk from a Fijian man I'd previously greeted on the street, so the smoke was flowing. Every evening, and a large chunk of the weekends, was spent chilling on the balcony of my apartment in the centre of Sydney, tumping away at our spliffs, and breathing in the lovely view of Sydney Harbour.

Seeing as it was quite a sizeable one-bedroom apartment, I slept in the bedroom and Chief slept on one of the sofas in the lounge.

One day, while I was at the office, discussing whether Fixed Assets should be written off over three or five years with the Head of Finance, I received a phone call from Chief.

"Wev. Wev. I can't open the safe."

"Really? Chief, I'm at work, mon. Just contact reception and they'll open it for you."

"But... the weed... is in the safe."

"Chief, I'm at work. Just deal with it."

With that, I put the phone down, apologised to my work colleague and returned to our not-at-all boring conversation about current assets, depreciation, nominal accounts, and how they should all be treated in their shiny new accounts system. I didn't hear anymore from Chief that afternoon and had completely forgotten he had called by the time I finished work. When I arrived back at the serviced apartments, I entered reception and noticed a few sniggers and odd smiles directed my way from the usually rude staff at the front desk. *What the fuck was all that about,* I thought. I rode the elevator up to the sixth floor and as soon as I entered my apartment, Chief sprang up from the sofa, ran over to the door ... and broke into nervous laughter.

"What's wrong with you?" I asked.

He passed me a lit spliff and told me to adjourn to the balcony, so that I could have a smoke as he told me the events of his day.

"Well, you know you told me to contact reception when I couldn't open the safe?"

"Oh, yeah. I completely forgot about that little phone call."

"Yeah. Well, I did."

"Alright..."

"Someone from housekeeping came up with a set of keys to open the safe and went straight into the bedroom to open it."

"OK..."

"Yeah. Well, I couldn't just let him open the safe, could I? There was an ounce of premium skunk weed in there."

"Yeah…"

"Well, he put the key in the lock, and was about to open the door to the safe, when I stopped him."

"What?"

"I stopped him. I put my hand on the safe door and told him he couldn't open it. He told me he needed to make sure the door had opened properly, but I told him he couldn't do it. He kept on insisting and I kept on telling him he couldn't do it. I kept my hand against the safe door, so he couldn't open it and he just kept on telling me that he had to open it."

"Right…"

"We were in a bit of a stalemate, so I just thought on my feet."

"Yeah, right," I laughed. "You can hardly stand on your own two feet, let alone think on them."

I took a drag on the spliff.

"Well, he wanted to open the door, to check it was OK, but I didn't want him to open the door, as it had a big bag of skunk in it, so I told him another reason he couldn't open the door."

"O … K…"

"I gave a little nod towards the bed."

"What?"

"I gave a little nod towards the bed and told him you had some… toys… in there. Dildos. Big dildos. And whips. I said he couldn't open it as it was a little embarrassing for you … and would he mind leaving the room, as I checked the safe door myself."

Imagine my face in this moment. I was fucking horrified.

"Yeah. He smirked and told me he understood, then left the room and let me open the door myself."

"You fucking cunt, Chief. I see him every day."

"Yeah. Really sorry about that, Wev. I just didn't know what to do. At least we got our skunk back, though."

I looked at my spliff, brought it to my lips and took a massive drag. I inhaled and exhaled slowly, as I collected my thoughts.

None of the apartment staff ever looked me in the eye again. They couldn't. I was the dildo guy in apartment 6F.

THE GANG

Before we slip further into my madness, I feel I must properly introduce the characters that have made my life so fruitful – my friends. Feel free to move on to the juicy stories if you wish, and ignore this section, but I felt it only right to shine a spotlight on these lovely lowlifes, and say thanks to them for making the highlights of my life so bright.

Being the fair chap I am, I have given them all the opportunity to sum me up in one sentence. Their description will precede my description of them (where I have allowed myself more than one sentence to describe them – it is my fucking book, after all).

First, honorary entries from my two kids:

Bubs: *"Dad's an absolute donkey with too many brain farts."*

Squiddles: *"Hola papá estoy en el 99 por ciento de mi caca."*

In absolutely no order whatsoever:

KOTCH

"Long Cat Stevens Syndrome."

Kotch was my gateway to the other drongoids I have spent my life of nonsense with. He is a six-foot-five beast of a man and has been through many different looks, from hip-hop gangster wannabe, to tie-dyed hippy, to steel-toe-cap-shoe'd hooligan, to Ian Anderson from Jethro Tull. He finally settled on the look of an extremely tall English-language teacher.

Kotch and I were best friends during my teen years. One

moment I will always remember Kotch by is when we were at Cropredy (a UK folk rock festival run by Fairport Convention). We were on mushrooms and Wadworth's 6X ale when I noticed a swarm of flies hovering above his head. We stood up, moved a good 100 metres from the swarm and sat back down. Within two minutes, the swarm of flies had caught his scent again and were back hovering above his head. Flies, like shit, love Kotch.

When I moved to London and started hanging out more with the likes of cocaine and heroin, our friendship drifted somewhat. However, as much as our outlooks on life diverged, our mutual love of stupidity has kept us in touch with each other to this day.

DANGER

"Wev is an old friend you feel like you've always just met for the first time."

Danger is another Dartfordian who I hung out with in my teens. We weren't massively close when we were younger, as I was a "suit" and he took an immediate dislike to that. I saw him as a pretentious university student. It took our increasing drug habits for us to sync and become best friends in our mid-twenties.

Danger is one of those people who when he can be bothered to try and do something he is invariably very good at it. He has a master's in art or philosophy, has published a book, written a screenplay, and would have become a successful musician (if he'd bothered to turn up to the contract signing with a major UK record label). He also nearly became a successful comedian, and is a great magician, chef and yoga expert.

Oh, and to top it off, while he was in his deepest, darkest heroin abyss, he set up a forum on the internet about lock-picking and is now the proud owner of a company worth millions, specialising in non-destructive entry mechanisms. When he was out of his head and just started up the company, he had the rozzers interested in what he was selling. They came round to his little studio flat to check out the merchandise. He had forgotten about this meeting and was busy smoking smack just before they arrived. He had to have a mad clean up (with the rozzers at his front door) before they came in and agreed a deal that had them purchasing lock picks that would help them perform drug busts. The irony.

Why is he called Danger? I have no idea.

NELSON

*"The only thing Wev has taken seriously
is not being serious."*

I've known Nelson the longest. We used to play football down his street when I was a boy, but I only really got to know him well when I moved in with him in Peckham and then Camberwell. He has childbearing hips and nipples the size of saucers. We always thought he was the "gay one" in the gang, but he has ended up married with two kids. Even my mother, Lin, was surprised when she found out he wasn't into cock.

Nelson was always a good one to take the piss out of during our hedonistic days, and he always took the constant abuse admirably. I think the amusement gained from being surrounded by such lunacy more than compensated for the continuous mocking hurled his way throughout our lives.

THE MULE

"Cunt."

The Mule is a non-Dartfordian. He worked with Nelson at a TV production studio in Soho and moved into our first pad in Peckham, when Keels moved out. He was pretty straight-laced when we first met him, only occasionally drinking. Within a couple of years, he had turned into a crazed coke head, alcoholic, paranoid schizophrenic. He also sported a massive ginger bouffant.

I lived with him and Nelson for years in Peckham and Camberwell and we were great friends. He was another one who I would constantly take the piss out of, but unlike Nelson, he couldn't handle it. Danger hated him and thought he was an idiot. My closeness to Danger pretty much ended my friendship with The Mule. Today, he won't even accept my friendship on LinkedIn. The bastard.

KEELS

"Gringo panthead."

Keels went to university with MJ and was living with him in Peckham, before Nelson and I were invited to move in from Dartford. He's a chunky, hairy Sikh, although being the second-born son means he doesn't sport a turban. That said, his brother also doesn't wear a turban, so it says a lot for his parents to allow their children the freedom to be who they are. And hang out with me.

Keels has travelled the world, working as an English teacher in Turkey, Kazakhstan, and Colombia. One of my favourite moments with Keels was turning up at his parents' house in Telford late one night, stoned out of our tiny little minds, to be greeted at the front door by his old man in his vest, stained y-fronts, and a pastel pink turban. An image I will never want to forget.

CHIEF

"Hairy, bald, smelly."

I've known Chief since I was 15. We both lived in Dartford. Chief is a bit of a genetic throw-back. His mother and father are white and English. Actually, his mother's skin colour is more trout grey, than white, but she's Caucasian, nonetheless. Chief, however, looks like a Cherokee Indian, thus the nickname. He's six-foot-six, with long, black hair down to his arse, giant hoof-like hands, a massive nose, and light brown skin. Nobody has managed to really get to the bottom of why there is such a discrepancy in skin tones between him and the rest of his family, but he is definitely not adopted; the older he has got, the more like his mother he looked (apart from the trout-grey pigmentation, of course). The best we have managed to come up with is that he had some Mongol ancestry sometime in the dark, distant past and has somehow picked up his skin colour through them.

Chief could not hold down a job, so he flitted between building sites, festivals, and the dole office for a living. I will always remember a CV he completed, while trying to get a job at a shoe shop Kotch used to work at. Under the section entitled "Education'" he answered "Yes" and under the section entitled "References" he answered, "My mum". There was also a time when he painted what he thought was "Hippy Revolution" in massive letters across his bedroom, only to be told by us better educated friends that he had spelled "Hippy Revulsion". These two little bits from his life sum him up perfectly.

BON

"If Boycie had a love child with a swerve ankle sloth."

Bon is the youngster in the group. We all have about 10 years on him. It is rumoured I would have seen him as a newborn, as my parents used to hang out with his parents when I was young. He's another giant, a man whose long arms mean that his knuckles drag along the floor when he walks. He was my best man at my wedding and gave a speech of approximately two words followed by stoned laughter. You can guess the two words.

Bon's another one that got crazily into drugs. I think him, Danger and I were the biggest fiends when it comes to our drug-induced escapades, which in itself brought a special bon(d) between us all.

MJ

"Generous, loving and smart, yet reserved, selfish and moronic. A settled escapist with hilarious adventures. Wevvy-woo is a complex simpleton."

MJ was funny when we were younger. He didn't want to admit that he came from the gutter and always aspired to being something that he wasn't. He tried putting on a posher accent than the rest of us and purchased a couple of second-hand Harris Tweeds, in the vain hope people would fall for it. He also had a disdain for his older brother, who we nicknamed "Mad Boy Malloy".

As we got older, and MJ stopped putting up a pretence, it became abundantly clear that MJ was the true "Mad Boy" in his family. He did us all proud though through his pub-landlord years, his boozers in Covent Garden, Soho, and Piccadilly became very convenient hangouts for us all on our nights out in London throughout our twenties. Where is he now? Folkestone.

OK, that's enough. Back to the stupid...

The wall that broke my fall

3.
THE FALL

When I was a teenager and lived in Dartford with my parents, all-day drinking sessions used to be quite a common affair. The Chug Chug Tavern was our favourite haunt. Unsurprisingly, the Chug Chug Tavern was positioned next to Dartford railway station, on a man-made hillock, that also housed council offices and a car park. On one side of this mound was a massive chemical factory that occasionally spilled not-so-nice things in the River Darent, that made it froth in a delightful piss-yellow colour. On the other side of this concrete knoll, was the infamous Dartford one-way system, which was the Le Mans for all boy racers in the area.

There were approximately 10 of us out drinking on this particular Saturday afternoon session. We'd take turns to pop out to the car park in pairs, smoke a spliff, then stagger back into the boozer, red-eyed, to continue our Löwenbräu-quaffing extravaganza. It was 4pm and we were about five hours, and 10 pints, into the proceedings, when one of my friends, Gibbon, asked me whether I fancied a spliff.

"Yeah, mon," was the obvious reply.

We stumbled out of the pub and walked across the car park to a knee-high metal railing that separated the car park from a steep grass verge, that then led to a wall, which in turn led to the bus stop on the one-way system below. We were pissed out of our heads by this stage, and it was quite windy. Gibbon pulled the skins and weed out of his pocket, and I got the tobacco out of mine. We fumbled around for a minute as the wind blew the skins and tobacco all over the place. There was absolutely no way we were going to be able to skin up. We both looked at each other and laughed. I just sat there perplexed at whether we should continue trying or whether we should just admit defeat and go back to the pub. Gibbon gestured to a small tree growing out of the grass verge, a few feet from where we were seated.

"Wev," he said. "Let's move along a bit and sit behind that tree. That should protect us from this wind."

I nodded and we both stood up.

The next thing I knew I was lying on the concrete pavement, next to some very startled bus wankers who were waiting for the number 96 to arrive at the bus stop far below where I had been just two seconds earlier. Somehow, standing up caused me to slip and fall approximately 20-feet down this grass verge, shuffle down 5-feet to the wall, then flip over the wall and fall another 15-feet, slap-bang on to the pavement.

I was unconscious when I hit the ground.

Gibbon woke me by slapping me around the face.

"Wev. Wev. You alright, mate?"

I tried to get to my feet, but quickly realised I couldn't stand up.

I then noticed a big pool of blood on the ground.

I passed out again.

I came round in an ambulance surrounded by a medic, Gibbon and Chief.

Over the next hour or so, I was in and out of consciousness and in and out of X-ray rooms. My bloodied jumper was ripped off me and was thrown into the corner of my hospital room. Chief told me he had called my parents and they were on their way to the hospital.

"Is it alright if we go when your parents arrive?" said Gibbon.

We then started hearing the screams of a crazed Liverpudlian woman in the distance.

"Where's me son?"

The screams grew closer. Louder. Intense. More annoying.

"Where's me son?"

"Wev. I think your mum's here," Chief said.

"I know that shriek anywhere," I replied sarcastically.

Chief and Gibbon went out to greet them and explained what had happened, then fucked off back to the boozer.

My parents both came into the room. Lin (I don't call her Mum) took one look at the sorry state I was in and screamed, "Me son!", then rushed over and held my hand. Dave (I don't call him Dad) looked at me and shook his head.

"I told you never to mix!" were his actual first words.

"What?"

"I told you never to mix alcohol and weed!"

Dave just stared at me with a look of deep disappointment and very little compassion. A couple of minutes later, a nurse came in with a massive surgical needle and a needle and thread. I took one look at the surgical needle and started shitting myself.

"We have to stitch up your head. You've got a nasty gash there."

I just mumbled.

"I'm just going to inject this anesthetic in your head, so you don't feel the pain when we give you stitches.

I nodded. Which hurt.

The nurse approached me. As she approached, I saw her squirt a little bit of the liquid that was in the needle up into the air. She grabbed my head tightly. I winced, closed my eyes, then screamed in pain, as the needle entered my skull.

The nurse rolled her eyes. Next came the stitches. She pulled the needle and thread out and started to work. All the way through this, I screamed in agony. My mother was in tears.

"Me son. Me son. Me poor son! You can see his brain. Dave, you can see his fookin' brain."

"Lin. Please calm down. He's alright," said Dave.

Then it was all over.

As the nurse started cleaning her stuff away, my mother turned to her.

"Is he going… to be OK?"

"He'll be fine," the nurse said. "He won't be able to walk for a few days, but we've X-rayed his skull and his back. Nothing's broken."

"Oh, me son … You could have fookin' killed yourself."

"When he fell, he landed on the base of his spine. That's why he can't walk. He then fell back and smashed his head on the pavement. He's lucky he was drunk; his body was relaxed when he landed. If he was sober, his body would have been a lot more tense, and we would have been dealing with paralysis."

"If he wasn't pissed out of his fookin' head, he wouldn't have fallen in the first place," said Lin.

"That's true too."

Dave looked down to me. "I told you never to mix!"

I made a full recovery. And thank my dumb fucking luck that I was shit-faced.

Days later, after leaving hospital, I was in the car with Lin and Dave and we drove by "Wev's Wall", as it is still called by a sub-section of Dartford's population, in honour of this particular escapade.

"That's where I fell," I recalled, proudly.

An expression of unbelievable terror filled Lin's face as she began to sob uncontrollably in the passenger seat.

4.
TATTOO ME

I t was the night before the eve of a new millennium, and my last night in Bethnal Green before embarking on a month-long trip to South America, that the lads billed as the "Dead Man Walking Tour". They decided to throw a party in my honour, as there was a distinct feeling that this was the last time we were ever going to see each other. Unfortunately, we couldn't source any cocaine or heroin for the gathering, so it was a night of skunk and Wodka (the Polish variant of vodka). I was particularly concerned that there wasn't any Class-A drug to accompany the booze and marijuana session. I had long ago learned that it was fine to mix alcohol and drugs, there just had to be a bit of Class-A action as part of that mix. Without them, there was always a risk of puking or falling off walls.

We were a few bottles into the evening when Danger produced a bottle of black Indian ink and a couple of needles.

"Shall we have a group tattooing session?"

"Fuck you, Danger!" was the unified response from the room.

"Oh, come on, you cunts. We're never going to see Wev again. It would be nice if we had something to remember each other by."

"Would you stop fucking saying that, Danger. I'm only going on holiday!" I said.

"You call going to Venezuela, Colombia, and the Amazon a holiday? You're dead, Wev. You're fucking DEAD."

Everyone nodded as if he had a point.

As his thoughts (not concern, I may add) for my safety rumbled around inside my compromised head, I decided that it would in fact be a lovely idea to have something to remember the boys by.

"Fuck it. Yeah, I'll do it."

"Fair play, Wev," exclaimed Danger. "What you going to go for?"

"I want an 'FP'" I said, not really thinking about it.

They all cracked up. "Fair play to the FP!"

Without any more thought or consideration to the sheer fucking stupidity of it all, I dipped the needle into the ink and hovered it two inches above my upper arm.

"I can't do it. I can't fucking do it."

I was terrified.

Danger laughed as he saw my fear. But he wasn't going to wait for me to pussy out. So, he stood up, grabbed the needle from my hand and stabbed it into my arm.

"Aaargh!"

It was the worst.

I closed my eyes tightly, and Danger set to work.

Stab, stab, stab, stab, stab.

There was a couple of seconds of calm, as Danger dipped the needle back into the ink, then stab, stab, stab, stab.

I screamed the bloody house down. The more I screamed, the more everyone just laughed.

"Wev. It's all over mate. I've done it."

My tense body instantly relaxed. I took a couple more lugs on a spliff, then looked at my arm.

"Hold on, Danger. That says 'EP'."

"No, it doesn't. It says 'FP'."

"No, it doesn't. Look. Doesn't that say 'EP?'"

The others looked at my arm. "It says 'EP'," they all cackled loudly.

"What the fuck does 'EP' stand for? It doesn't fucking stand for 'Fair play'."

"Don't give me any shit, Wev. I did my best," said Danger, trying his best to look serious through tears of laughter.

I looked at my arm again. There were trickles of blood and ink rolling down my arm.

"For fuck's sake, mon. Right. Danger. Come on. Your turn."

Danger's face of high amusement suddenly became one of deep concern.

"Fuck that, Wev. I ain't going through any of that shit."

The rest of the group agreed.

"It was a stupid thing to do, actually," said Danger.

So, there I was. The lone tattooee, sitting there with what looked like "EP" scrawled on my arm. It looked as if had been done by a drunk, dyslexic toddler, which in hindsight it probably was. I ended up finding a tattoo artist on a skanky market stall in Venezuela who nobly corrected Danger's mistake. It still looks shit. Just a little less shit.

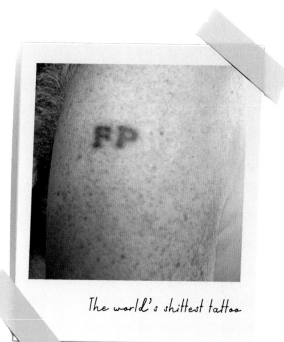

The world's shittest tattoo

The Kong before the storm!

5.
TYPHOON VALIUM

Mid-2003.

A typhoon was fast approaching Hong Kong and a Signal 8 warning was raised by the authorities. This meant that everyone needed to get back home and bolt themselves indoors as soon as possible, as all schools, shops, transportation, and workplaces would be shut down until the storm passes. The gusts of wind can get up to 180 kilometres per hour, so it's pretty dangerous being outside when one of these fucker's strike.

It was a Saturday morning, and we were all at work in the Central District on Hong Kong Island. One of my work colleagues, Teddy, asked me if rather than me sitting in my apartment alone when the typhoon struck, I would like to spend the lockdown with him and his wife at their apartment in Discovery Bay, Lantau Island. He informed me that he had a stash of Valium, ripe for consumption. He had previously managed to blag them off an NHS doctor by informing him that he was terrified of flying and needed to do the gruelling 12-hour Hong Kong to London flight on a regular basis. He also informed me that he had a couple of bottles of vodka on ice. I didn't need much persuading after that little piece of information.

We managed to get the last ferry to Discovery Bay and walked to his apartment. Discovery Bay is a small collection of apartments and villas on Lantau Island, one of Hong Kong's outlying islands. Very few Hong Kong Chinese lived here, as it was a purpose-built expat community. The only vehicles that can be driven around this place are golf carts. And seeing as these are the only vehicles allowed, the price to buy one of them is ridiculous. I was never really a fan of Discovery Bay and, in general, I am not a fan of these gated havens for expats that you find dotted around the world. But I can see their attraction and understand why people love living in these insular communities. A home away from home. There is a fish and chip shop there, a kebab shop, and the local supermarket, stuffed full of produce you could buy in a shop in the UK (although about five times more expensive).

When we entered his apartment, Teddy's wife, Sarah, greeted us with a large glass of vodka orange each. We made a pile of sandwiches and sat around the table on the balcony, drinking and munching. It wasn't raining or particularly windy at this point, so we managed to have a very pleasant 30-minute exchange of niceties about nothing in particular. After getting a little bored with the conversation, I decided to pipe up.

"Come on then, Teddy. Where's the Valium?"

"Oh yeah. I'll just get it."

Teddy disappeared into the bathroom. He returned with a box of diazepam. He opened the box up, prised two shiny blue tablets out of the packaging and handed them to me. He then offered another two pills to Sarah. She was a sensible young lady, so declined the offer. Teddy and I both giggled like naughty school children and downed them with a couple of swigs of vodka. There was no turning back now.

Valium makes you act like a right donut without you realising you are acting like a right donut. Valium, with the addition of alcohol, accentuates the general donut-ness of your actions tenfold. Sarah knew that what was in store for her that evening, was a couple of blokes with slurred speech and a distinct lack of coordination, who thought they were 100 per cent coherent, so she stood up, took a couple of sandwiches and her vodka, then went back into the apartment, leaving us drongos sitting there, chuckling away to ourselves on the balcony.

Teddy and I sat laughing as the clouds darkened around us and the sea below us grew rougher and rougher. It was only 4pm, but it felt like it was midnight. The wind and rain started kicking in seriously. Teddy and I sat there, spaced out, as the palm trees that lined the beach got battered and bent horizontal by the storm. It was pretty full on. The rain started blowing in our faces and our clothes quickly got soaked through as we vegetated on the balcony in our state of sedated bliss. Sarah called out to us both.

"Why don't you both come inside? It's dangerous out there."

"We're big boys," Teddy called back.

We sat there for another 30 minutes, gibbering shit, and watching the craziness of the storm, then had another Valium each. Teddy suddenly stood up.

"I need a piss. I'll be back in a minute."

Teddy went in the apartment. I heard a few murmurs of conversation, then silence for a minute, then a few more murmurs of conversation.

"Wev. I think you should come inside. It's really dry in here."

"Is it? Wicked. I'm soaking wet."

I picked up our glasses of vodka and made my way into the apartment. As I entered, I knocked into a couple of pieces of furniture. Sarah jumped up and guided me to the safety of the sofa. I handed Teddy his glass of vodka. He handed me another Valium. We spent the next couple of hours, watching the local news on TV that was reporting about the damage the typhoon was wreaking across Hong Kong and Southern China. By 8pm, the worst of the typhoon had passed, and the Signal 8 warning had been lifted. Teddy turned to me.

"Shall we down another couple of Valium and go for a walk?" asked Teddy.

"That, my friend, is a fantastic idea. Let's do it."

"Wicked. I'll pour some vodka into this empty water bottle, so that we don't go thirsty."

Sarah shook her head with dismay. "Are you fucking serious? You could both die out there."

Teddy eased her fears.

"It's alright, love. I'll call you if we get into any trouble."

"You're both idiots. Fucking idiots."

With that truth ringing in our ears, we both left the apartment and meandered down to the central plaza of Discovery Bay. We saw that there hadn't been much damage, apart from a few upturned bins, so decided to walk up the hills that overlook Discovery Bay, in a search for destruction. We followed the pathway from the central plaza to the top of the nearest hill and sat on a bench that overlooks the town.

"Shall we have another Valium?" Teddy asked.

"I was thinking exactly the same thing."

We swilled two more pills down with gulps of vodka orange.

"Shall we pay a visit to the Trappist monastery?" Teddy asked.

"What the fuck is a Trappist monastery?" I slurred.

"I ain't got a clue. But I know there is one on the other side of these hills and have always wanted to visit."

And away we went. We turned left down some track. The track wound its way through a forest. The general state of our heads by this stage made the shadows and shapes of the trees quite interesting and a little nerve-racking. I popped into the bushes for a piss. Within 30 minutes we saw the silhouette of a small white building, hidden amongst the foliage of trees and bushes. We assumed it was the monastery but by that point, neither of us cared. We faffed around for a few minutes, then realised we were both being quite loud.

"Shall we just get the fuck out of here? I won't be able to handle it if a monk comes out," Teddy said.

"What do you think a Trappist monk looks like anyway?"

"I ain't got a clue. I don't even know what religion a Trappist monk is."

"Neither have I. Do you reckon they look like little Smurfs?"

"If they do, I don't really think I could handle being approached by a little Smurf at this particular moment, so let's just get the fuck out of here. Head to the beach."

I nodded in agreement. I was in no mood for little blue creatures.

We left the monastery behind us and trundled further down the track, until it reached a small cliff face, with a pile of rocks that led down to the sea. Teddy had previously insisted the track would have led to a beach that would in turn lead to Discovery Bay.

"Where's the beach then, Teddy?"

"Er, I think it's a bit further along."

We looked in the direction of Discovery Bay. There was no way we could walk along the top of the cliff face, as it was covered in thick bush.

"All we have to do is climb down on to the rocks below. Can you see those rocks over there?"

"There are loads of friggin' rocks, Teddy."

"Those ones over there. About 100 metres away. I think that's where the rocks end and the beach begins. Once we get to those, we'll be able to walk along the beach back to my apartment."

"You sure about that, mon?"

"Yeah. The beach starts just over there."

With that, we took another deep swig of the vodka, then started clambering over the rocks. It was quite a nervy experience. The rocks were all wet and the waves were strong, spraying us every couple of seconds with the salty, polluted water that surrounds Lantau Island. After slipping a few times, we finally got to the rocks that Teddy had pointed out. We could now see the lights of Discovery Bay, but it was still quite a distance.

"Ted? Where's the beach?"

"Er, I think we must be a bit further along than I'd thought."

I rolled my eyes.

Teddy pointed to somewhere in the distance.

"I reckon if we get to those rocks over there, we'll be alright."

We continued scrambling and jumping over the rocks until Teddy stopped.

"Shit."

"What?"

"We can't go any further."

"What?"

"I can't get to the next rock. There's just a 20-foot drop down to the sea now."

I caught up with him, and looked down at the predicament we now found ourselves in. There were waves crashing violently 20-feet below us and the next rock we needed to reach was a good 5-feet from where we were standing. I was not going to attempt jumping that.

"Right. We'll just have to go back the way we came."

"Let's have a quick drink of vodka first," I said, appreciating the scenic view.

We took a swig each, then started the long clamber back along the cliff face. We made it about 20-feet back across the rocks, till we came to another sudden stop.

"Shit."

"What?"

"We can't go any further."

"What?"

"The tide must have come in. I can't see any rock to jump on to."

"Shit," Teddy confirmed.

We were stuck.

"What the fuck do we do?"

"I don't know."

We both sat down on the rock. And laughed.

"Friggin' hell. We are a couple of wallies," I said.

"I'll call Sarah. She might be able to help."

"Good idea. I don't fancy being stuck here all night."

Teddy called Sarah and explained what had happened. I could hear quite a lot of shouting down the other end of the phone and felt extremely happy that I was a single man. Suddenly, the barking on the other end of the phone stopped and there was silence.

"Shit. My phone's run out of battery."

"No worries, mon. I'll lend you my phone."

I rummaged around inside my pockets.

"Hold on. I can't find my phone."

"What?"

"I ain't got my phone. I've either left it at your apartment or it fell out."

"Shit."

We sat there in a dazed silence for a few moments. We were in the middle of a raging storm, and were stuck on a rocky precipice with no way back.

"Well, er, let's just hope Sarah sorts something out then."

The next hour or so was spent quenching our thirst with the remnants of the vodka orange and wondering whether we were going to sit perched on top of this rock for the rest of the night. It then started raining.

I was panicked, but only because the vodka had ran out.

Then, we saw a helicopter ascend from Discovery Bay and climb into the cloudy, dark night sky. It slowly made its way over the town and out to the sea. Once it was over the sea, a beaming light came out from the bottom of it.

"Do you reckon that's looking for us?" I asked.

We both stood up and watched as the helicopter flew in circles around the bay. After more than 30 minutes of it searching the sea with its spotlights, it started beaming its brightness along the coastline.

"I think it is looking for us," Teddy said. "I think Sarah must have called for help."

The beam of light started edging closer to us and eventually was directed at us two sorry twats, waving our stupid hands above our dumb heads.

"We're here. We're here!" we shouted as if the helicopter could hear us.

The helicopter hovered for a few seconds, then flew over the top of us and into the hills and forests behind us.

"Shit. Do you reckon they saw us?" Teddy said.

"I thought so."

"But why the fuck have they gone?"

"I ain't got a clue. Maybe they've going to get some ropes to lower down and rescue us."

"Over the friggin' forest? Nice place to keep ropes."

Ten minutes later, an even brighter light beamed at us from the sea. A rescue boat.

"What the fuck is that?" I said.

"I don't know, but it's hurting my eyes."

Next thing you know, there was this voice booming through a loudspeaker.

"We can see you. We can see you. Stay calm. We will send some people over to help. Just wait there."

We both laughed. "We ain't going anywhere, mon."

The boat edged very close to the rock we were standing on. We could see some men in helmets, playing around with some ropes. One of them climbed on to the edge of the boat, then started descending to us numpties on the rock. He managed to make it to a couple of the rocks that were closer to the sea. Luckily, he was wearing waterproofs, as the waves were crashing around him. The waves didn't seem to bother him at all, and he climbed up to the rock where Teddy and I were standing with minimal fuss.

"Right," the rescuer shouted. "We will take you onboard one at a time. Come to me."

He produced a life-jacket from his bag. He grabbed one of Teddy's hands, then somehow managed to put the life jacket on Teddy with his other hand. Another man then attached a rope to it, pulled and fiddled around with it for a minute, then shouted through his walkie-talkie. Teddy was thrown into the air, bumped into the side of the boat a couple of times, then dangled his way to the safety of the deck.

"OK. OK. You now."

The rescuer grabbed my arm, as the life jacket was lowered back down from the boat. He put the life jacket on me, and I was then lifted into the boat. The other man followed soon afterwards. There were about five to six crew members in the boat. They gave us the once over and asked us what we were doing out on the rocks.

"Er, we got lost," I said, highly intoxicated.

As the boat started making its way back to Discovery Bay, I turned back and realised that the helicopter was still hovering over the forests behind the rocks where we were previously stuck.

"What's the helicopter doing? You've rescued us. They can fly home now."

"No, they can't. There are 10 police officers in the forests, trying to find you. The helicopter is guiding them back to the road."

Teddy and I looked at each other, half-embarrassed, half-impressed.

The rescuer looked at me with utter disdain.

I looked at my saviour and felt deep emotions well through my fucked-up soul. I approached him and hugged him and I whispered in his ear.

"I love you."

I'm pretty sure I could feel him roll his eyes.

6.
NIPPLE FLAP

I looked over at Marcy, blood dripped from her left tit on to the clean meeting-room floor. "You've bit my fucking nipple off. You wanker! You've bit my fucking nipple off!"

"Fuck. I'm sorry, Marcy," I said, lying naked on the table in Conference Room A at the offices of my work. I was in excruciating pain. Blood dripped out of my mouth. Marcy ran out of the room screaming.

This palaver all started when, after imbibing a few harmless beverages in a pub in the City of London, I had the bright idea of sneaking back to my office so Marcy and I could take advantage of the free supply of champagne they had on offer in the fridge that serviced the many meeting rooms they had in the lower ground floor. It was around 10pm, so nobody would be around, and I had a key.

What could possibly go wrong?

We finished a bottle of champagne and shared a spliff in Conference Room B, then decided to have another spliff and bottle of champagne in Conference Room C. One thing led to another and within minutes, I was laying back on the table in Conference Room D, in a world of pleasure.

Marcy, a work colleague of mine for several years, was a keen fellatio benefactress and had found a very willing fellatio beneficiary in me. I writhed around in bliss for what seemed an eternity, until I thought I was going to blow my load.

"Woah. Hold on, mate. Not yet…." I slurred. I pulled myself away from her and decided to return the favour. I laid her on the table and soon had her wriggling across the meeting room table, like an epileptic slug.

Marcy moaned, "Fuck me, Wev. Fuck me!" and being the generous fellow I am, I obliged. I slid on top of and inside of her and started doing my thang. A few minutes into our mutual love fest, Conference Room D's table creaked, then crashed down to the floor, with us two numpties crashing down on top of it. Somehow, I remained lodged inside of Marcy. I asked Marcy whether she was alright, and she just cracked up laughing. "I think we got a bit carried away there, didn't we?"

We both stood up and looked around us. The meeting room was a mess, with table legs, the table, clothes, and a spilled bottle of champagne, strewn across the floor.

"Come on then, let's find another room," said Marcy.

We walked out into the main reception area, and both feasted our eyes on the 20-foot beast of a meeting-room table in Main Conference Room A.

"That's the table for us." We gave the table a few shoves until we were satisfied it was sturdy enough, then climbed on top and continued what we had started. Everything was very pleasurable and going as these sorts of things tend to go, until Marcy dug her nails into my back.

"Fuck, Marcy. That hurt."

"Don't stop, Wev. Fuck me."

I tried to ignore the pain and the fact that I was aleady fucking her. Again, she dug her nails in.

"Marcy. That fucking hurts!"

"Shut up. Keep going."

Again, I ignored the pain. She dug her nails in a third, fourth, fifth and sixth time. The pain was severe, but I decided to just struggle on through it. ("SOTI" for those of us in the know). When she dug her nails into my back for the twelfth time, I thought I had to try to take my mind off the pain she was inflicting on me, by nibbling away at her nipples. This was an unbelievably bad move, as when she dug in for the thirteenth time, I was mid-nibble and clenched my teeth down on her nipple. Immediately, I could taste blood, and as I felt around with my tongue, I noticed her nipple was at a very different angle to what it was seconds earlier. She threw me off, and ran screaming into the toilet to assess the damage.

When Marcy returned, she showed me her nipple. The poor little thing was hanging off the breasts, flapping painfully. There were two big gashes, one at the top and one at the bottom, where my teeth had sunk through her flesh. It was hanging on to the rest of her tit, by two slithers of skin either side of the bite wounds. After assessing the damage, we decided to call it a night and got a cab back to my pad in Camberwell.

On reaching my pad in Camberwell, we both got undressed and into bed. When I took my white shirt off, I saw that it was drenched in blood, from the various scars she had given me. The front of her shirt had a little pool of blood, where her nipple was still bleeding. We both looked at each other sadly and agreed that we'd had enough carnal pleasure for the night, so slept in each other's arms, both feeling particularly sorry for each other and ourselves. I felt frigging terrible for having bit her nipple off, but also felt that she had sort of brought it upon herself.

When we woke the following morning, my bed sheets were covered in blood. I looked at her nipple, with its open wound still looking raw, and told her that she needed to go to the doctors the next day. Nobody at work was aware of our little office romance, so I went to work so as not to arouse any suspicion, and unfortunately couldn't go with her. I spent the morning, unable to lean back on my chair, as the pain that shot through my back was intensifying and meant I couldn't concentrate on anything. Around midday, Marcy called me to let me know that the doctor had applied a couple of butterfly stitches and had advised her to tell her boyfriend that – *and this actually happened* – "he should wear a gum shield the next time you have sex".

Awkward.

7.
DEAD CAT

One night during my LSD-fuelled teenage years, I was out in Dartford with Kotch and another friend, Reg. It was around 10pm and we were on our way back to my parents' house for a hip-hop binge. We had spent the day down the local park, drinking booze, smoking ganja, and tripping our nuts off on acid.

As we turned on to my parents' street, we were confronted with a dead cat in the middle of the road. It freaked us all out a bit but intrigued us enough to study it a bit closer. As we nervously approached, we realised that the feline was in full-on rigor mortis, with shit coming out of its arse and vomit coming out of its mouth. It was rank. I really felt sorry for the poor bugger and thought that even though it was dead, it still needed a bit of respect and to be taken out of the road, so that it won't be squashed to a pulp by more passing cars.

I looked back down at the cat, thinking about how we could potentially move the dead fucker to somewhere else. I then noticed something horrific.

"Shit. It's my neighbour's cat."

Kotch looked at me in horror. "What?"

"It's my fucking neighbour's cat. I can't believe it. It's little Scrubby. They're going to be gutted."

"Shit, man. What are we going to do?"

"I think we've got to get it out of the street and put it in his front garden."

"What?"

"Come on, mon. I can't leave Scrubby in the middle of the

road to be run over again. The least I can do, is stick it on their pathway, so they can give him a proper burial when they find him dead in the morning."

"Fuck that, Wev. Just throw it straight in the bin."

We all laughed. We then all agreed on my idea of getting Scrubby out of the street and respectfully placing him in the front garden of my neighbour's' house. We scrambled around the street and in a few gardens looking for a spade or something to pick the cat up with. After making a few curtains twitch, with our general hubbub, Reg found a spade from a garden shed a few doors down. He proudly brought it out and handed it over to me.

"Oh, nice one, Reg. So what? I'm the one that has to scoop the fucking thing up?"

"Yeah. It was your idea, and it's your neighbour's cat."

Grimacing, I walked over to Scrubby and scraped the spade under his cold, lifeless, stinking body.

"It's stuck to the fucking road."

"What?"

"I can't get the spade under its body. Scrubby's stuck to the road."

My thoughts of a respectful burial were now replaced with thoughts about how I got myself into this situation and how I could end it as quickly as possible. I forcefully shoved the spade under the flattened carcass.

With a crunch and a scrape, and the disjointing of a few limbs, Scrubby was finally on the spade. The shit and the vomit emitting from the cat's orifices had solidified, which meant that as I lifted the spade up, Scrubby's head and arse were being pulled down to the ground by the vast volumes of putridness that had previously exited its body.

Kotch and Reg stood a few steps back and started to laugh. I decided to give the spade a bit of a jolt and thrust movement. After a flash of concern that Scrubby's head and arse were going to separate from the rest of its body, they set themselves free of the concrete. Finally, I was now standing there with a newly liberated Scrubby.

I walked over to the neighbour's house and placed the dead cat in the garden. As I turned to leave, another pang of guilt entered my mind. I couldn't just leave Scrubby there, for my neighbour to open his front door in the morning as he popped over the road to buy his Sunday newspaper and find his Scrubbster dead as a doorknob on his doormat. That wouldn't be right. I had to tell him that I'd found him with his head smashed in by a car, in the middle of the road and that unfortunately, his dear Scrubby was no more.

I knocked on the door. Kotch and Reg went on the missing list. Cunts. I knocked on the door again. I heard a shout of "Who is it?" coming from the other side. I told him it was me. He shouted for me to hold on, then opened the door in his pants and vest (looking a tad pissed off to have been disturbed at this time of night).

"Hello, Wev. What do you want?"

The gravity of the moment came crashing through my soul and I was lost for words. The neighbour looked at me intensely. I then remembered that I was out of my fucking mind on drugs, and it would be obvious to anyone that looked at my stupid face.

"Err..." I pointed at dead Scrubby on the ground. The neighbour looked at dead Scrubby, then looked back at my face. A face that screamed, "Look! Look what I did to your cat."

"W-w-w-what?" he blubbered, as tears started streaming down his eyes. "Yeah, sorry, mon. I found him in the street and thought you should know."

I handed the shell-shocked man the spade, covered in his beloved cat's guts, and bolted.

It was never spoken of again, but I know – *I know* – that my neighbour just assumed the worst based on the only evidence he had: I killed his cat for sport while I was fucking high out of my mind, and then, in the middle of the night, gave the dead body to him as some sort of evil trophy.

8.
GANGS OF NEW YORK

When I was working at the travel agents in Chinatown – circa 1998 – I won two free flights to New York at a Chinese New Year raffle sponsored by work.

I gave my second ticket to Chief. MJ, The Mule and Nelson decided to join us for the two-week trip.

We had been there for a few days and had done the typical tourist things, such as sing "Working Class Hero" where John Lennon was assassinated and got pissed up on the top floor of the World Trade Center. Things were getting pretty desperate on the ganja front though, to the point where I started asking anyone on the street that looked like a stoner whether they had any weed. No luck.

During those first few days in New York, I had noticed however that there was always a gang of 10-or-so geezers who seemed to be constantly hanging around on the street corner not far from our hotel. I decided to grab hold of Chief for a bit of moral support and approach them. I noticed a couple of them were smoking blunts.

"You alright there, G-dog?" I said, immediately regretting that introduction. "I'm from London and looking to score some ganja. Can any of you chaps help me out?"

They all looked at me as if I was a terrorist.

"Come on, lads. Do us a favour and sort us out with a bit of weed."

There were a few chuckles, then one of them said they could sort us out. I handed him $50, and he put his hand in his pocket to complete the transaction.

Out of nowhere came the distinct sirens of a New York squad car. As it pulled up at the kerb in front of us, the gang scarpered down different streets and alleyways, and Chief and I ran back to the hotel. Thirty minutes, and a change of clothes later, we went back to the same spot to find that the gang of 10 had now become a gang of nine. I asked where the geezer with my money was. I was greeted with lots of laughter.

"You won't see him or your money again," they said, as they pointed to some stairs that led to the subway.

I lost the plot. I told them all that they had to sort me out with the herb then and that I would refuse to leave until they had sorted me out.

"Wev. Calm yourself down, mate. You'll get us in trouble."

"I don't fucking care. I gave one of their mates 50 fucking dollars. He's fucked off, so it's down to them to give us some weed."

I was livid. I was adamant that I wasn't going to leave until the remaining gang members had recompensed me for my loss. I started barking about how this wouldn't happen in London (it does and has), that they were fucking cunts, and there wasn't any of this black-white divide type shit going down where I lived. Just harmony. The gang found this quite amusing, then eventually three of them told us to follow them down an alleyway. Chief and I stood up and as we were walking down the alley, I thought we were finally getting somewhere and that we would be justly rewarded for our persistence.

I proudly exclaimed, "We're just like you, you know, mon. Don't fucking skank us."

One of them was highly offended by that comment and got right in my face and shouted, "You're not like us." He then gave me a shove.

I stumbled back a couple of yards then shouted back at him. "We're from London. We're not some idiot tourists you can just rip off."

Chief then jumped in and said, "We ain't fucking idiots."

Just then, the situation intensified. The geezer who pushed me, then pulled a gun out of his pocket. "Your money's gone."

He pointed the gun at my face. But I remained defiant.

"Just give us our fucking weed, mon. I'm not leaving without it."

The three of them just looked at each other and cracked up laughing. "These are some fucking crazy mother fuckers!"

All of a sudden, the mood relaxed.

The emotional one put his gun back in his pocket and snatched a blunt out of his mate's hand and handed it to me "Have some of this, you crazy fool!"

Chief and I caned it within a couple of minutes. We followed them back to the street corner and sat back down on the pavement. I promptly started back up again, informing them that I was most grateful for the top-quality blunt, but I wasn't leaving and would stalk them until I was given my money back or given a nice bag of weed.

The three members started muttering between themselves when, out of nowhere, we were approached by a couple of ladies. Sorry, hookers.

"Do you want some fun, boys?" they said, approaching us and rubbing their fingers together.

"I give the best BJ in New York," one of them exclaimed. Chief and I looked at each other. We didn't doubt it.

"We would love to, but we ain't got any money," I responded. "Those guys have run off with it. If you want to give me a blow job, you'll have to get my money off them fuckers."

The hookers and the gang members cracked up. This last comment must have hit home, as the moody gun boy walked back over to me and pulled out a small bag of weed. "Take this, you crazy fucker. Now get the fuck outta here, before I change my mind...."

I said sorry to the hookers, then Chief and I made our way back to the hotel, skipping along the street in remarkably high spirits. I was over the moon. I managed to score the weed I paid for and, most importantly, didn't get shot for being a dumb, and arrogant, shit.

Lewisham Station in the 16th century

9.
FLYING PUKE

When I was still living in Dartford with my parents, the lads and I would regularly go out on the razz in London. The train home would always be interesting, as this was in the days before there were bogs on suburban trains. Drinking and needing a piss every 20 minutes was a constant throughout my booze days. The journey from Central London to Dartford is 45 minutes. This little predicament of weak bladder and longish journey tended to result in either trying to rush off a train, piss against a platform wall and get back on the train before the train left or, even worse, pissing out the window of a moving train. Again, trains were different back then. You used to be able to open the window of the train door. I think they stopped putting windows in doors, as too many people got their cocks chopped off, whilst pissing in the wind. However, this one journey home gave me more than I had bargained for.

I had met Kotch immediately after work and drank a skinful of ales, on an empty stomach. As the train trundled down the tracks from London, the jolting up and down started making me feel a bit sick. I told Kotch, but he just cracked up and told me that I was a lightweight. I thought that maybe I should just try to sleep, so that the lump that was forming in my stomach would just disappear. This was a bad move, as closing my eyes led to a whole heap of head spinning and the ascendancy of the lump in my stomach to my throat. I thought I was going to vomit, but I had to try to keep it down, as there was nowhere to vomit.

The train carriage was empty, so I curled up on the seat in a foetal position, with the vain hope that this would make me feel better, but it didn't help either. I was in a right state. Kotch just sat there pointing at me, laughing. He then stood up, pulled the window of the door down, slapped his cock out, and pissed out the window of the train. Splash back from the wind, threw a few droplets of piss in my direction, but I was in too much of a mess to get out the way of the shower.

As he finished pissing and put his cock safely back in his jeans, he turned to me and told me to just be sick out the window. Knowing that his cock had been dangling there 10 seconds earlier, and there was bound to be a load of piss dribble over the train door, I refused to comply. I thought that I'd rather lay there in a state of sickly inebriation, than be drenched in more Kotch crotch fluid.

I closed my eyes again, but my head started spinning out again. I thought I was going to throw a whitey, so opened them up, and just felt the sick rising and rising.

"I don't think I can hold it in. I might just vomit on the floor."

"You can't vomit on the floor, you dirty prick. Just puke out the window."

"You've already drenched me in your piss. I don't want to stick my head anywhere near that window."

"Don't be such a knob, Wev. You'll feel better once you've been sick. Just make sure it's out the window, as I don't want to look at or smell your puke for the rest of the journey."

"Argh. For fuck's sake, mon. I feel rough as shite."

"Just fucking puke out the window. Your groaning is doing my head in, and you're starting to make me feel sick."

"Argh. Fucking hell…."

"Just vomit, you stupid cunt."

As Kotch's final words on the matter rang through my head, I bolted up to the train window, stuck my head out, and vomited. It came gushing out. It felt like pints of the stuff, came flowing out of my mouth.

As it started gushing, streaming, leaking, a terrible sight greeted my eyes. The train was moving slowly through New

Cross Station at the very instant the puke came bursting out of my mouth. The initial gush hit a man on the platform straight in the face. There was a woman standing a few metres further down the platform. Her face, eyes and hair got plastered – properly drenched – in that opening surge of puke. Another man, a few metres down from her, got away lightly, as he just got splatted with a few chunks from the initial vomit. Two blokes, standing together talking, were rudely interrupted by the second stream of bile and barf. This was, fortunately for them, stringier than the first wave of sick, so they were only hit with long streaks of spit across their faces and not the full-on vomit that the first two poor fuckers were hit with.

Luckily, for me, the train didn't stop at New Cross, and sped me safely back to Dartford, leaving those poor souls to deal with the aftermath of their brush with Wev's Water without me. I will never forget the look of panic, confusion, and unquenchable anger, on the faces of those people. As the train pulled away, I was deeply sorry for what had just happened. But when I told Kotch, and he started to cry tears of undiluted joy, I too saw the funny side.

Bellenden Road, Peckham (Had to be done)

10.
BIN-BAG NAPPY

I was invited to a house party in Wimbledon by a girl called Alison, who worked at the same property company I did. She told me that I could invite some friends, so I decided to bring Nelson and The Mule, my flatmates from Peckham. Nelson and I had moved from Dartford to Peckham with MJ in the mid-90's, and had picked up The Mule on the way, as he was working with Nelson at some TV production house in Soho. The Mule had previously led a sheltered life in a large house on the outskirts of Colchester, so hadn't really drunk or taken drugs before meeting me. As such, he was a lightweight.

The three of us jumped in a cab from Peckham to Wimbledon, stopping off at a local off-licence first to get a few beers for the party. We rocked up to the house and knocked at the door. Alison answered, invited us in and offered us all a glass of rather punchy rum punch.

We imbibed away and mingled with the other 30 or so guests. Most of them weren't really the type of people I would hang out with, as we came from a different spectrum of the social ladder, but there was quite a nice, relaxed vibe to the party, and we were having a good time. After an hour or so of heavy drinking and light mingling, Nelson and I caught sight of The Mule.

"Wev," Nelson began. "I think The Mule is pissed."

The Mule was caressing the curtains in the front room. We walked over to him.

"Mule Boy. What the fuck are you doing?"

"Nothing. I'm just stroking the curtains. They're... nice."

"Alright, mate, but you might want to leave them alone and

come and talk to a few people."

"Alright then," The Mule slurred. "But I'm going to grab another rum punch. It's really good. I don't think it's very strong, as I've drunk quite a lot of it. I would have thought that I'd be pissed out of my head by now, but I feel alright."

"Fine. Just stop fingering the curtains," Nelson said.

Nelson and I left The Mule to the rum punch; we started talking to the other guests again. As we got back into our conversations, we completely forgot about The Mule.

Twenty minutes later, we spotted The Mule back over by the curtains. Not on his own this time. He was busy stroking the curtains with his left hand and fondling the hair of a girl with his right hand. Nelson and I laughed but left him to it.

As the evening progressed, The Mule disappeared. We thought he had gone for a snog-and-tickle with the girl he'd been gibbering to earlier, so didn't think too much of it. I was then approached by a genuinely concerned Alison, the party's host.

"Er, Wev?"

"Yeah?"

"Your friend is in the toilet and, er, he won't come out."

I laughed. Alison didn't.

"Really?"

"Yes. And lots of people need to go to the toilet. Can you please get him out?"

Nelson and I walked to the top of the stairs and brushed past a queue of desperate toilet-needers.

I went to open the toilet door. The door was locked. I knocked on the door.

"Uuuuuhhhhh…"

An uneasy noise echoed from within.

"Mule. It's Wev. You have to get out. People need to go to the toilet."

"Uuuuuhhhhh…"

"What are you doing? Let us in."

"Uuuuuhhhhh…"

We waited a few seconds. Nothing happened, so I banged on the door again.

"For fuck's sake, Mule Boy. Get out the fucking toilet!" bellowed Nelson.

"Uuuuuhhhhh…"

This time, I heard a bit of shuffling around, then a fumble around the door handle.

The door opened ever so slightly.

I turned to the increasingly desperate people in the queue. "Give us a second," I said. "We'll just make sure he's OK but will get him out as soon as possible."

They all gave us sheepish smiles but nodded in agreement. Nelson and I then proceeded through the toilet door. The Mule was keeled over the bath, retching.

Nelson and I laughed.

Come on, you twat. We need to get you out of the bathroom. There's a queue of people outside."

"Uuuuuhhhhh…"

The bath was full of vomit. OK, maybe not full. But there was a lot. Chunky stuff. It stank.

"Oh, for fuck's sake, Mule!"

I grabbed the toilet brush and began squashing the vomit down the bath plughole. It seemed to go down OK. I gave the toilet a quick wipe and a flush for good luck, ran the shower around the bath, then picked The Mule up and put his arms around our shoulders.

"You ready?"

"Uuuuuhhhhh…"

We carried him out. As soon as we opened the door, the first person in the queue shoved their way past us and into the bathroom. They hurriedly locked the door behind themselves; as we pushed past the queue, to the top of the stairs, I heard a groan. The smell was bad, but a new problem had presented itself.

"Shit, man. These stairs are steep," I said to Nelson.

We adjusted The Mule's positioning on our shoulders, took

a breath, then leaped forward off the top of the staircase and…
effectively cartwheeled down the stairs as a trio until we landed
in a heap at the bottom of the stairs. In my head, it looked cool.
To observers, it probably looked like three grown men tumbling
downstairs, using each other as support.

Nelson and I looked at each other in astonishment at how
that manoeuvre played out. The Mule dropped his head on my
shoulder and started dribbling. Alison was waiting for us at the
bottom and was in fits of laughter as soon as we reached her.

"What?" I said, amazed to still be alive, dusting myself off
from Nelson and The Mule.

"Your friend's jeans – they're round his ankles."

Nelson and I looked down and saw that The Mule's jeans were
indeed round his ankles. We both cracked up too. After a couple
of minutes of pointing and laughing – and it was minutes – I
decided we needed to put the poor Mule out of his misery.

"Nelson, can you pull them back up for him?"

"Can I fuck? You do it, Wev."

"How can I? He's leaning his head on my shoulder and dribbling down my chest. I'm just about keeping him upright."

Begrudgingly, Nelson got out from under The Mule's armpit,
bent down to the floor and pulled The Mule's jeans up. He then
did the zip up, so that they wouldn't fall down again.

"I'm not doing that again," Nelson grimaced.

"I think we're going to have to take him home, ain't we?"

"Yep. Alison, can you order us a taxi, please? I'll leave The
Mule out the front, whilst we wait."

I didn't want to leave The Mule in the house just in case he
was going to vomit again, so I opened the front door and went
out into the front yard. To the left was a collection of four full
bin bags. I dumped him with the rubbish and went back inside.
Alison ordered a cab.

Ten minutes later, we heard a toot from outside. It was the
taxi. Nelson and I said our farewell and apologies to Alison and
the other people we'd socialised with that evening, and went out

the front door. The Mule was laying asleep amongst the bin bags. We picked him up and carried him to the taxi.

"Uuuuuhhhhh…"

"We're taking you home, mate. We're just getting in a taxi."

"Uuuuuhhhhh…"

We all got in the back seat of the taxi. The Mule in the middle, with Nelson and I either side of him. The driver turned to us.

"He looks a bit worse for wear. Where are you going, lads?"

"Ha-ha. Yeah. He had a little bit too much rum punch. Er, can you take us to Peckham Rye please, mate?"

As I said this, I could see the taxi drivers demeanour transform, and take a turn for the worse.

"What. The. Fuck. Is. That. Smell?"

"What?"

"It smells like someone's shit themselves."

Nelson and I both turned to The Mule. The smell hit us both instantly.

"Get the fuck out of my taxi. Now!"

"Shit. Sorry, mate. We're really sorry."

"Get the fuck out."

Nelson and I jumped out, then pulled the soiled Mule out of the taxi.

"What the fuck, Mule Boy? You've fucking shat yourself!"

"Uuuuuhhhhh…"

We looked at the back of his jeans and could just see a shit running up The Mule's back and through his jeans. The smell was hideous.

Back in Alison's front garden, we returned The Mule to his righteous place amongst the bin bags outside the house.

"What are we going to do? No taxi is going to take us back to Peckham with him stinking like that."

"I don't know, mon. We'll think of something. Let's ask Alison to order another taxi."

We knocked on the front door. Alison answered with a confused expression on her face.

"Er… The Mule has shat himself."

"What?" she gasped.

"He stinks of shit and the taxi driver threw us out of his taxi."

"Oh. What are you going to do? He can't come back in here."

"Can you order another taxi, please? We'll sort something out."

Alison ordered another cab. "20 minutes."

"Right. 20 minutes to sort this shit out," I quipped.

I needed a piss, so I went upstairs. The queue was only one person long by this point, so I managed to get my slash in, without much waiting time. Whilst I was in the bathroom, I noticed there were lots of shampoos and body washes around the bath and on the shelves. I picked up a couple of bottles of shampoo and took them downstairs. I found Alison talking to a few people in her kitchen.

"Alison? Do you mind if I use these shampoos to hide the smell? I'll pay you back. And do you have a spare bin bag?"

Alison just laughed hysterically and nodded.

I found Nelson. Both of us went out to The Mule, who was unconscious still on the bin bags. We squeezed the contents of the shampoo bottles all over him, carefully ensuring we covered the length and breadth of his body on the floor.

It was at this point I realised how drunk I was.

"Now he smells like a combination of papaya extract and… shit," I said.

We carefully smothered it into The Mule's clothes a bit, being very conscious not to soil our hands with whatever evils lurked beneath his jeans. Just to be safe, we propped The Mule up and made him wear a bin bag like a nappy.

"Right. When the taxi comes, we'll just have to make sure we open both of our windows and chain-smoke all the way to Peckham. Hopefully, that will mask his smell."

The taxi arrived right on time. We picked The Mule up and carried him to the taxi. We shoved him into the middle of the backseat, then sat either side of him. Before we shut the doors, we opened the windows.

"Can we smoke in here, mate?" I asked the taxi driver.

"Yeah. No problem." It was the nineties, after all.

Nelson and I both lit up a cigarette each, then shut the doors.

"Peckham Rye, please," I said, resisting the urge to say. "And step on it!"

"Alright then."

And off we went. The shower-gel-shit-bag camouflage worked. The next 30 minutes were spent shivering in the wind that was blasting through the back windows. As we neared our location, Nelson came up with the bright idea of getting the taxi to park around the corner from our flat.

"You know, Wev. If he's left a massive stain on the backseat, I don't want the cabbie to come knocking on our door."

"That ain't a bad idea, Nelson."

We instructed the taxi to stop around the corner from our pad. When the cab stopped, the driver turned round to us all.

"That'll be 25 quid please, lads."

Because he's a cunt, and he thought it would be funny, Nelson opened the backdoor of the cab and bolted out as fast as he could and ran straight off into the distance. He left me to not only pay for the taxi, but also get The Mule out on my own, without the taxi driver getting suspicious of why he was dressed in a bin bag and smelled of papaya extract and shit.

"Keep the change, mate," I said as I handed the driver 30 quid and dragged The Mule out of the taxi.

We got The Mule into the house and on to the sofa. In the morning, I couldn't help but feel sorry for him when he asked, "Why am I wearing a fucking bin-bag nappy?"

It was the least of his problems.

Dog meat restaurant, Hanoi

11.
DOG'S DINNER

Christmas Day, 2003.

I was all alone in Hanoi, Vietnam. Somewhat weirdly, after the rather peculiar experience of viewing Ho Chi Minh's embalmed corpse in the morning, I was hungry. So I decided to have lunch at one of Hanoi's *thịt chó* restaurants. *Thịt chó* restaurants serve dog meat. Vietnamese people have eaten dogs for years and to some people, it is as normal as eating chicken. There are also some who believe that eating dog at the end of the month will wash away all the bad luck that was gathered in the weeks beforehand. I'd had a particularly bad month, so thought I'd see whether it was true. I had previously paid a street urchin $50 to be my friend/guide for a few days – that sounds weirder than it actually was, and not worthy of a story itself – so I informed him of my wish to eat a dog. Not because I am a psychopath, OK, but because I am curious about all of life's peculiarities. He told me there was a good restaurant on the road out of town. We jumped on his motorbike and rode to the restaurant, picking up a couple of his friends on the way.

The restaurant was a rickety wooden shack on stilts. My three Vietnamese friends and I stumbled up some stairs and into the shack. A small, sweaty, skanky woman with a moustache followed us up the stairs and had a couple of minutes conversation (in Vietnamese) with my rent-a-friends. She then picked a booger out of her nose, looked at it, then wiped the sweat from her moustache and left. I asked them what was going on. They said they had asked her to give us a selection of her best dishes. Within a couple of minutes, I heard a few dogs barking. A bad sign, I thought. I then heard a clank of metal, then a very loud death yelp. A few more clink-clanks of metal were heard, a couple more whimpers, then silence. My friends looked at me and smiled.

"Dinner."

Within 20 minutes or so, Sweaty Tash Woman, as I nicknamed her, stumbled back up the stairs and presented us with four plates piled with different types of salad leaf and some chapati-style bread. I had a nibble of the salad. My friends stared at me.

"No! You not eat now. You eat with meat."

I stopped eating the salad. Another five minutes or so later, three to four dishes were served to us. These were the beginnings of the feast. I sat there, unsure what to do. My Vietnamese friends sat there, motionless.

"Do we eat now?" I said.

"No. Wait. More food come."

"OK..."

Two to three more dishes came out. There was then a quick bit of jibber-jabber between my friends and the Tash, then she turned to me proudly.

"Eat!"

I was unsure what to do with this plethora of canine culinary delights, so waited to see what my friends would do. They picked up a chapati each, put some salad on it, selected a dish, scooped some of the meat on top and scoffed it all up. The dishes were basically various cuts of the dog that had just been brutally murdered for my eating pleasure, and that had been cooked in several different ways. Some looked like pieces of meat in a spicy sauce, some looked like a cheap cut of lamb and some looked like an abortion. None looked or smelt particularly appetising. Seeing that I was not heartily tucking in, they all turned to me and said "Eat!" in unison. I felt I now had no choice but to follow their lead.

Pun intended.

Dog meat tastes a lot like chewy lamb. I'm unsure whether it was chewy because my brain was telling my mouth that I shouldn't be eating this shit, but the combination of hound, strong-smelling leaves that tasted a bit like coriander, and chapati went down better than I expected. One dish tasted a lot like black pudding. I didn't ask, and didn't want to know if the dish was congealed dog blood, but I ate it and sort-of enjoyed it, nonetheless. After we ploughed through all the food, Sweaty Tash Woman came back, collected the empty plates and bowls, turned to me on her way out and gave me a toothless grin.

"Soup?"

"Yes?" I replied, wondering what I had just let myself in for.

A couple of minutes later, she returned with a big metallic bowl – not a dog bowl, thankfully – and placed it in the middle of the floor. In the bowl, was murky water, a sprinkle of herbs and four boiled... dog legs.

She scooped some of the muddy water and a dog leg into the bowl and plonked them down in-front of us. My friends picked up their allocated dog leg and started gnawing away. I picked my dog leg up and stared at it. There was hardly any meat on it at all. Just a fingertip's worth under the knee, maybe. The rest was bone, cartilage and what was clearly a dog's paw on the end. I took a nibble of the meat. I tried the bone and cartilage combo. It didn't really taste of anything, but, even if it had, I just couldn't stop glancing at the dog paw.

Many years later, when my children asked for a pet, we got two cats. I'm not sure I can look a dog in the eye anymore.

12.
WEDDING CRASHER

An elderly Kurdish woman came stomping over to me in a rage. "I have warned you on a number of occasions. Turn this rubbish off."

"What? But this is BDP. A proper tune."

"It is just noise. Turn it off and get out of here now."

"This is a big hit in all of the clubs in London and New York."

"You are a 16-year-old child," she said, still enraged. "What do you know about clubs in London and New York? Have you ever been to one?"

"That's not the point," I said.

"Listen. If you don't turn this off now, I will call the police."

I looked around me. The hall was full of other elderly Kurds, sitting at tables around the dance floor in varying states of shock, anger, and tears. The only people who were dancing were my fellow DJs, Kotch and Reg, who were throwing themselves around in a pissed-up version of Michael Flatley's *Riverdance*. Our friend, Kalvin, who got us the gig, came over to join the argument.

"Wev. Please leave, mate. You have ruined my sister's wedding. Unless you have any different music, you need to go. You really don't want to get my mum or my family any angrier."

"Really? But I thought you liked hip-hop?"

"I haven't got a clue what hip-hop is. I just knew you lot gibbered about it a lot and that you had a radio station that played it. I didn't think it would sound like this."

(We did have a radio station called Jade FM that played solely hip-hop music, but due to it being broadcast via a CB antenna, meant that the catchment area for potential listeners was restricted to my parents in the front room and my next-door neighbour's dead cat.)

"Just turn it off!" shouted his mother in disbelief.

"OK. OK," I grabbed the microphone and announced, "Kotch. Reg. We have to turn off the music. It ain't quite hitting the mark."

Kotch stopped dancing and shouted, "No... I thought you were going to put NWA on next."

Forgetting I was still speaking through the microphone, I replied, "Yep. 'Fuck the Police' is a no-go, mate."

At this point, there was a noticeable gasp from the bride, who then proceeded to burst into tears. The loud song finally came to a quiet end and then there was silence. Kalvin told his mother to get a tape of some Kurdish music from her car so that they could put it on instead. I stood there, very disappointed at the unfortunate and unexpected turn of events.

"Kalvin, mate. I really don't understand."

"Wev. You are pissed out of your head. How can you not understand? Look at the people here. They are all old and from Kurdistan. Do you really think they would have liked the tripe you lot have been playing all night?"

"Well, I thought that because hip-hop artist's sing about oppression and the Kurds have been oppressed, there would be some mutual understanding."

"Just pack your stuff up, Wev, and get the fuck out of here... before my uncles show you what oppression really is."

Me, Kotch and Reg begrudgingly accepted our fate and started packing our stuff away. Kalvin's mother returned with a cassette tape. "How do I put this on, son?" He advised her that cassette tapes won't work on record decks and that she should ask the bar staff whether they had a tape player hooked up to their speakers. Kalvin escorted us out the door. As we walked towards the exit, the Kurdish music came blasting out through the bar's speakers. All the wedding guests cheered, stood up in unison and started strutting their stuff on the dance floor. We had at least brought the family together, I thought. Even if it was in unity of their hatred of our music.

Outside, I turned to Kalvin. "We're still getting paid for tonight though, aren't we, mate?"

"Fuck off, Wev. You've drunk shitloads of free booze, ruined my sister's wedding and upset my mother. You're lucky I'm not punching you right now."

And that was the beginning – and end – of my DJing career. Thank fuck.

Not Zelda

13.
SEX CCTV

A few of the lads and I were on an all-dayer with the landlord, landlady, and a rough old trout of a barmaid we nicknamed Zelda, from the Chug Chug Tavern in Dartford. The barmaid was nicknamed Zelda due to her likeness to an ugly character of the same name in *Terrahawks*, an eighties' kids' TV show. (To be fair, our Zelda had a lovely personality.) If you are unaware of this particular show, please do a Google before proceeding with the rest of this story. I ain't bragging.

We all ended up getting really pissed, then stumbled back to the Chug Chug Tavern in the evening. As we were all happily imbibing away, Zelda approached me and asked whether I fancied having a game of pool. I was never a big pool player, but thought, *Fuck it, why not?* The door to the pool room from the bar was locked, so she told me to follow her through the bar and in via a different entrance.

After a couple of games, Zelda made her move. I had just finished taking a shot when she pounced on me. I was trapped between the pool table and a slobbering space monster. I still had the pool cue in my hand and managed to push her away with it.

"It's your shot, isn't it?" I said. She grabbed the pool cue, stuck it on the table, then pounced again. This time the slobbering was accompanied by a vigorous rubbing of my cock and balls. I pushed her away again. Admittedly, with a lot less gusto than my first attempt to prise her off me. Her hand continued to fondle my cock, but I at least managed to wench her head away from mine.

"We're in the boozer, Zelda. I don't think we should be doing this."

"Don't worry, Wev. The door to the bar is locked and the landlord and landlady won't disturb us."

I started thinking that this entrapment had been pre-arranged with the landlord and landlady. As my mind started running through the idea of being stitched up, Zelda had managed to slip my cock out of my pants, with a swift and impressive bit of hand movement. It only took a couple more rubs before I gave into the slobbering monster and became a slobbering monster myself. I unbuttoned the top few buttons of her shirt and flopped one of her tits out so that I could slurp around that, whilst I hitched her skirt up and started playing around with her damp, flabby flange. She then hoisted me on to the pool table and slavered all over my knob's end.

The beer goggles had kicked in hours earlier so Zelda the Alien Witch had magically turned into a semi-fit MILF, even though this was the early nineties and MILFs weren't even invented back then. I was loving it. I looked down at the beauty who was gnashing away between my legs and thought, I just have to have her, and I have to have her now. I pulled her up and positioned her on the pool table beside me. She let out a little scream.

"Ouch!"

"What's wrong?"

"The fucking pool cue. It's right up the crack of my arse."

I laughed, then moved her off the pool cue, and rested her sagging arse cheeks on to the edge of the pool table. I then positioned myself in front of her, hoisted her skirt up a bit more and slipped my cock through her steamy forested mess and into her dark pit of despair. I started thrusting myself back and forth. She leaned back on to the pool table, with one tit bouncing around out of her shirt and the other safely tucked away inside.

As I started to think I was about to reach my climatic goal, Zelda jumped off my cock and began sucking me off once again. Seconds later, I shot my load over her face and hair. Not deliberately, I must say. It's just where it landed.

About a minute later, after I had wiped my cock on my shirt, and Zelda had cleaned her face, and popped her boob back into her bra, I heard a rustle of keys and a knock on the door that led to the bar. The door started opening, so I grabbed the pool cue that was still on the table and span around as if I was about to take a shot at a non-existent ball. I heard a roar of laughter coming from the bar.

The landlord came in through the door with a big apologetic smile on his face.

"I'm not sure how to explain this to you, but the whole of the bar has been watching you both on the CCTV."

"What?"

"See that camera up there? Well, it's on, and it displays every-thing that is happening in this room on a TV in the bar."

I looked at Zelda in horror. As she smiled back at me, her MILF-esque looks disappeared back to that of a haggard puppet woman. I was devastated.

The landlady piped up. "I'm so sorry. We were going to stop watching, as I didn't think it was fair that you didn't know what was going on. But we didn't…."

I buttoned my jeans back up and left the pool room. As we entered the bar, we were greeted to a combination of cheers and laughter from the 20 blokes who had experienced the whole sorry affair. If it's possible to feel shame and pride at the same time for the same event then I did, and thankfully Zelda seemed unfazed by it all.

The night didn't end on a sour note, though. Both Zelda and I managed to get quite a few free beers from a few of the blokes in the bar, as a thank you for the entertainment we had provided.

"Good shot," one of them said, raising his glass, and bursting into laughter.

Taking the piss again

14.
PISS HALLWAY

I woke up naked and hungover to fuck. My mouth was as dry as a nun's vagina, and my head was pounding, no doubt like a nun's vagina. I put some clothes on, edged out of bed, and fell over some garden-chair cushions.

"What the fuck?" My head didn't understand what the cushions were doing in my bedroom, but was too tender to try to calculate how they had got there.

I stumbled up the stairs to the kitchen for some headache tablets, water, and a cup of tea. As I reached the top of the stairs, I heard a mumble from the front room. It was my old man, Dave, with a facial expression that flitted between amusement and disappointment.

"Alright there, Dave?"

"Humph," he humphed.

"OK. Do you want a cup of tea?"

"Humph."

"I take that as a no, then."

I went in the kitchen wondering what the fuck that little bit of interaction was all about, downed two paracetamols with a large glass of water and made myself a cup of tea. I faltered my way into the front room and collapsed on to the sofa. Dave, who was watching whatever shite tended to be on TV on a Sunday morning in 1992, glanced at me, smirked, and went back to staring at the boredom that was on the box. I sat there, desperately trying to get my head back to some sense of normality. I felt fucking terrible. After 30 minutes of the occasional sneer and "humph", from Dave, Lin came in.

She greeted me with a "Hiya, love."

"Morning, Lin."

"You alright, son?"

"Not really. My head is killing me."

"It's not surprising, you were in a right state last night."

"I don't remember anything about last night to be honest."

Dave interjected. "You're lucky, you don't remember anything."

"What? What do you mean?"

"Humph."

"Eh? What does that mean?"

Both of them chuckled to each other, then looked at me with a distinct sense of displeasure. My mother asked whether any of us wanted a cup of tea, then collected our mugs and shuffled into the kitchen. I looked at Dave, confused. He ignored me and turned to the TV again. My head was still killing me, but I knew something was up. I just didn't have the energy to try to work it out, and I didn't have the energy to push the conversation further with him.

Soon I could smell some piggy getting fried up, and within 10 minutes Lin entered with a pile of bacon sangers and a fresh brew. Dave and I fought our way through the pile of sandwiches, finished our teas, and smoked cigarettes. My head started feeling so much better after that. I picked up the newspaper, checked out the football scores from the previous day and tried to spark up a conversation with my parents about the results and what that means for West Ham and Charlton's positions in the league and how that affected their respective push, for promotion to the Premier League. Again, I was greeted with nothing but a "humph".

This was now starting to do my head in. What the fuck was their problem? Now that my head was feeling a bit better, I decided to confront them.

"Dave. Can you just tell me what's wrong?"

"Humph."

"Oh, come on, mon. You're starting to do my head in."

"You really want to know? Lin? What do you think? Should

I tell him?" Dave said, half laughing.

"Oh, go on, Dave. Just tell him."

They both looked at me with that weird smirk of annoyance again. It was so strange. Amusement and anger in the same facial expression. My head was spinning with confusion.

"Yeah, Dave. Just tell me."

"You pissed in the hallway last night."

"What?"

"You pissed in the hallway. Do you remember coming in pissed last night and being a nuisance around Lucy?"

"What are you talking about?"

"My work colleague, Lucy?"

"Yeah. I know who Lucy is. What about her?"

"She was here last night."

"Was she?"

"Yeah. And you came in pissed out of your head and started flirting with her."

"Did I?"

"Yes. You were acting like a right prick. She got really embarrassed and I had to send you to bed."

"I don't remember that at all."

"Yeah. Well, as I said, you were pissed out of your head."

"OK, but what's that got to do with pissing in the hallway?"

"Well, I'm coming to that. A couple of hours after you had gone to your room, I was taking Lucy to the front door to say goodbye and as we were walking down the stairs, you came running out of your bedroom door, stark naked."

"What?"

"You ran down the hallway naked, shoulder-barged the wall, then stood in the hallway pissing."

"Fuck. Really?"

"Son. Please don't use that language around us," cried Lin.

Dave continued: "You must have heard us when you were pissing in the hallway, as you turned around, looked at us both in horror, then ran back to your room, grabbing the cushions from the garden chairs to wrap around yourself, as you ran."

I looked at Dave and then to Lin. "We had to mop your fucking piss up," said Dave. "I didn't sign up for that."

"And I'll have to throw away those cushions," said Lin. "Or burn them."

To this day, I still don't know how –or why – those garden cushions were in the hallway, but thank fuck they were.

15.
CINNAMON FUN

The following story took place during the COVID-19 lockdown in our undisclosed location. It probably seems a little out of place, amongst all the hedonistic stories of my youth and is more applicable to the planned "Family Edition" book, but I thought it should be included in "Volume 1", so you, my friend, can clearly see that just because I am now a bald, old cunt with a family, the stupidity continues. It also comes with a warning that I think every man should be aware of, before they make the same dumb-shit mistake as me.

My wife, KT, and I are quite into essentials oils. My wife likes them due to the health benefits you supposedly get from them. I like them because they make smelly me smell nice.

KT makes soaps, lip balms, and all our house cleaning products out of them. She does this so that we don't get polluted with the rank chemicals that come with modern-day cleanliness. I always add a few drops of essential oils into my nightly bath.

Anyway, one night I gave my daughter, Bubs, the opportunity to choose which oils I should add to my bath. She selected cinnamon and sweet orange then scurried off to spoon it with my son, Squiddles, in bed. I started the bath, got undressed, and sat on the toilet for a quick slash, whilst the water was running. Once I'd finished, I washed my hands, then picked up the bottle of sweet orange oil. I unscrewed the lid and added a couple of drops to the bath, no problem.

I then wanted to add the cinnamon oil too. I unscrewed the lid and tipped it upside down over the bath. Nothing came out. I gave it a shake, then tried again. Nothing came out. I then tried shaking it, whilst holding it upside down over the bath. Again, nothing came out. I held the bottle up against the light. There was only a little bit of oil left so it was too shallow to come out of the plastic contraption that drip feeds the oil out of the bottle. I decided to take the drip thing off and pour a few drops in the old school way. This worked a treat.

I put the drip thing back on again and in doing so, noticed I had a pool of concentrated cinnamon oil left on my thumb. I thought about plunging my thumb in the bath water but saw steam emanating from it, so thought it would be too hot to dip my digit in. I then caught sight of my extremely well-endowed member in the bathroom mirror.

Why don't you have a posh wank? I thought. I can strap myself off and my knob will be left with a lovely cinnamon scent afterwards. Everyone's a winner.

I leaned back against the cistern, separated my legs, started thinking about Zelda from *Terrahawks* (just joking), then began the wank-a-thon. All was going well and, extremely, pleasurable for the first couple of strokes, then a painful heat started rising from my cock. The sensation and intensity doubled with each wave of pain. I must have rubbed the essential oils all over, and into, the entire surface area of my genitalia. From base to tip. And surely some had leaked inside.

"Fuck, fuck, shit, shit, bollocks! It's burning. It's fucking burning!" I screamed out loud.

My knob was throbbing, but not in the good way.

"Fuck it. I've started, so I'll might as well see this through," I said to myself.

I managed to struggle on through the pleasure-pain barrier and when the time came to cum – boom! – I ejaculated hot molten lava. The burning pain shuddered up and down my knob, as the globules of spoof fired on to my gut.

Almost immediately, my cock went from an erect and proud soldier to a poorly worm, and flopped down on to my scrotum. This led to not only my cock feeling as if it was on fire – a burning

I cannot even describe to you, dear reader – but my balls also felt they were being ironed too. The essential oils must have leaked on to the poor chaps.

I turned the cold water tap on and frantically started patting my cock and balls down. This increased the pain, as I still had some cinnamon oil on my thumb and was just applying more to the affected area. I grabbed a towel and started dabbing it, but that didn't work either. I looked at the bath: that was too hot to just jump in.

Luckily, we have more than one bathroom in the house, so I ran out of that bathroom and straight into another – a trail of smoke and the smell of singed hair, cinnamon, sulphur and burnt skin emanating from my nether regions (that description may be a slight exaggeration, but it's definitely how I remember it). I jumped into the shower and put it on full blast, aiming the shower head directly on my inflamed cock and balls. Unfortunately, this shower was on full heat, so yet again, tears rolled down my cheeks with the burning sensation I was experiencing.

Once the freezing cold water flowed freely, I just stood in the shower shaking and sweating, and allowed the pain to subside. At this point, I was truly worried about the long-term damage to my penis.

I have never used essential oils in my bath since – and neither should you.

An idiot abroad

16.
MILE HIGH

Being a ganja fiend and working as an IT professional has its pros and cons. Obviously, the pros revolve around having a good salary, and therefore a fair old amount of disposable income, to fuel my habit. The cons (apart from having to actually work for that disposable income) revolve around the amount of travel this role tends to encompass. In my role as IT Director in Hong Kong, I was travelling regularly around Asia and Australia, and would have to try to source my beloved herb at each new destination, so that the business trips were less depressing. And, as you may know, drug dealers don't exactly advertise their services.

Before my first and only business trip to Singapore, I did a bit of research on the internet and found that their drug laws were some of the strictest in the world, so my normal trick of walking up to strangers and asking for assistance in sourcing ganja for me, was most likely going to prove unfruitful, and would also risk getting me into quite a bit of trouble.

I was travelling to Singapore with my colleague, Teddy, and as we had an early flight, we could go straight to the airport from the office. I was in mental turmoil as to whether I should take a small lump of hashish with me, as I was only going to be in Singapore for two nights. Half of my brain was telling me to just do it, as I wouldn't need to carry much, so it could easily be concealed on my body. The other half of my brain was telling me not to do it, as I didn't want to end up in some sweat pit of a prison. I finally decided to take a small lump and stash it in my suit jacket pocket, so I could dispose of it easily, if the need arose.

The flight from HK to Singapore went without any suspicion, despite my intense paranoia for the whole flight. I had a couple of Singapore Slings to calm my nerves and to stop me from looking like the exact type of person who would smuggle drugs on a flight.

Teddy and I landed in Singapore Changi Airport at midday. We passed through passport control and approached immigration. Paranoia started coursing through my veins. I looked around me and felt the stares of the officials, burning through me, and burning through my suit pocket, containing my little lump of hashish.

I decided to come clean just in case I was pulled over. "Ted, I've got a lump of hashish."

"You what?"

"I decided to bring a little lump of hash with me, as I knew I couldn't score over here."

"You fucking prick." Teddy gave me a look of petulance.

"Don't judge me, mon."

"I will fucking judge you. What the fuck are you doing bringing that with you?"

"You know I can't go a night without a little smoke. This is for when I am back at the hotel."

"You idiot, Wev. I ain't going to help you. If you get pulled over, I'm going to carry on walking and will go straight to the office."

He was right. But, still, what a cunt.

We got closer and closer to immigration and I just knew I was going to be pulled over. The officials were staring at me with stern looks. Teddy refused to look at me, and started walking faster, to get as far away from me as possible. I started sweating, through sheer fear. I put my hand in my pocket, grabbed the hashish, stuck it in my mouth and swallowed it. I really couldn't risk getting arrested on a business trip. As we reached the immigration desks, I started my guilty trudge towards the officials, looking at them expectantly, but at least now safe in the knowledge that they won't find any illegalities on my person. As I approached the desk, I started unzipping my laptop bag, and was only stopped when I heard Teddy.

"Wev? What are you doing?"

"Eh?"

"Come on. Keep on walking."

The immigration officials looked at me and smiled but didn't ask to search my belongings. I looked at them and a thought flashed into my mind. *Hold on, I've just eaten a lump of hashish and you cunts don't even want to search my bags? Fucking wankers.* I veered away from the officials and caught up with a very dis-illusioned looking Teddy. I looked at his increasingly impatient head, and another thought crossed my mind. *Hold on. I've just eaten a lump of hashish and I'm now going to the Singapore office for an afternoon of corporate bullshit.*

We walked out of the airport and got in a cab to take us to the office. Teddy turned to me.

"I bet you feel really proud of yourself now."

"Not really."

"Hope your smoke tonight is worth it."

"Well actually, Teddy, it won't be… because I ate it."

"You did what?"

"I fucking ate it. I got paranoid and just stuck it in my mouth and swallowed it."

"Won't you be fucked at the office?"

I shrugged my shoulders. "Sometimes it can come up strong and sometimes it can be a few hours before you feel anything. I'm going with the hope that I won't feel anything until after we've left the office."

Teddy nodded his head in despair. He refused to speak to me for the rest of the journey to the office.

When we arrived, I just tried to forget about the hashish. Teddy and I reached reception and were greeted by Rick, one of the staff that reported to me. Seeing as it was around midday when we arrived, they had arranged a spread of food and juices in one of the meeting-rooms, and led us there. Rick handed us both a plate and told us to tuck in. As I started filling my plate with culinary delights, the hashish kicked in. I started feeling lightheaded and dizzy, so I made a beeline directly for a chair and sat down with a thud. Teddy and Rick looked at me. A knowing smirk came across Teddy's face, but Rick had a look of concerned surprise. I could feel sweat forming, and my vision started going a little blurry. Rick offered me a watermelon juice, which I gratefully accepted. I downed that and requested another. As Rick went to pour me another glass, I sat there thinking, *Sort it out, Wev. Sort it out.* Teddy sat there smiling and shaking his head. I mouthed a "Fuck you!" to him, and he mouthed the same back at me. When Rick came back with another juice, I apologised to him, saying that I hadn't been feeling well over the last few days and didn't get much sleep the night before, so might not be on top form. Teddy scoffed loudly.

We finished our food and drinks, then Rick told me he was going to beckon in a few of the senior members of the team in, so that I could demonstrate the centralised property database we had developed for them.

My world collapsed around me.

How the fuck was I going to be able to keep it together? I could hardly talk. I said to Rick that he should tell them that I wasn't feeling well, so it may be better if we had the meeting the following day. If possible, could we change the afternoon's session to be Teddy talking about all of the technical and hardware requirements that will be needed to host my shiny new centralised property database? Rick told me he would see what he could do and left the meeting room. As soon as the door shut, Teddy looked at me and said, "What the fuck are you doing, changing the agenda at a moment's notice?"

"Ted, mate. It's one of the perks of my role."

"You prick."

"I think you'd better start getting your presentation together."

"You fucking prick."

Rick soon reappeared and told us both that the changes I requested were fine with everyone and that everyone would soon be in the office for Teddy's presentation. The relief that went through my soul was immense. A few minutes later, five people had entered the meeting room. Each time, I had to stand up, shake hands and exchange niceties. And each time this happened, it became increasingly more difficult, as my head was a total mash up. The incoherence in my speaking had now extended to an inability to use my legs to a standard required for walking. I just constantly repeated my mantra of, "Not feeling well. Might be something I ate. Will feel better tomorrow." They must have been wondering what the fuck was going on with this IT Director from Head Office.

Teddy started his presentation, and I went deeper into a tripped-out stupor. Fortunately, I wasn't called upon to provide much input for the rest of the day, so just sat there, focusing on the end of my nose, whilst they all focused on the model professionalism that emanated from Teddy. As soon as the demo ended, I told everybody in the room that I had to leave immediately and that I'd see them in the morning, as I was going to the hotel to lie down. They said that they understood and that they hoped I felt better in the morning. I managed to stand up, edge outside and hail a cab, then spent the remainder of the evening tripping out in my pants on the hotel bed, until I fell asleep at around 7.30 pm.

I never got stoned at work ever again, I think. To be honest, I can't remember.

Sunday funday down the local Hut

17.
PIZZA HUT

Back in the late eighties, when I was an underage drinker and boozers in Blighty weren't open on a Sunday afternoon, the lads and I would regularly pop down the Chug Chug Tavern at 11am, drink as many pints as we could fit in, and munch on the free salted roast potatoes that were on offer, until 12.30pm. After which, we would get around the licensing laws, by going on to Pizza Hut for a Peroni and all-you-can-eat pizza session, until the Chug Chug reopened around 7pm. Pizza Hut was our choice of venue, as not only was it able to sell booze, but one of our friends, Creak (who later became a world-famous actor) worked there and would always throw a few freebies our way.

One Sunday, just as the Chug Chug was closing at 12.30pm, me and three of my friends (Kotch, Chief, and MJ) and I realised that I was the only fucker with any money left.

"Shit. We can't go to Pizza Hut."

"No worries lads, I've got some dollar. I'll front it."

We all stumbled down to Pizza Hut and spent the next three hours raucously imbibing a cornucopia of libations and munching down on the stodge fest that is a Pizza Hut all-you-can-eat buffet. Feeling as if I'd had enough of the festivities, I suddenly stood up.

"Nice one, chaps, I'm off. See ya down the boozer later."

I downed the dregs of my bottle of lager and marched out of the restaurant, chuckling to myself. It then dawned on the lads that they didn't have the means to pay for the food and beer we had been swilling over the last few hours. They therefore decided to stand up and throw the table in the air, spilling beer bottles and pizza crusts across the floor, then run out the restaurant laughing.

They caught up with me in the street, about 50-feet down from the restaurant. We all congratulated ourselves on our stupidity and then agreed to meet down the pub in an hour's time. Kotch went home. The rest of us stumbled into a police van and four unhappy police officers. We were all manhandled, pushed into the back of the meat wagon and driven to the police station. It was while in the back of the police van, that I remembered I had some LSD in my train pass wallet.

"Shit," I said quietly to myself.

I managed to sneak the wallet out of my jeans pocket and stuffed it down my underpants before we got out the van at the police station.

Luckily, the rozzers must have been feeling generous that day, as we managed to get away with two hours of sitting alone in separate cells followed by some fingerprint taking and an "official" caution. We all left the police station laughing but decided to call it a day and went back to our respective homes. As I was walking back to my parent's house, a thought flashed past my lips.

"Where the fuck is my train pass?"

I frantically started searching my pockets, trouser legs, and shoes. It wasn't there. Shit. It must have somehow wound its way out of my underwear, down my trouser leg and into the back of the pig's van.

Bollocks.

The following day, I went to the train station and got a new pass. I told them it had got stolen.

The rest of the week then continued much like any other week, and nothing untoward happened.

The following Saturday, the lads and I were in a local graveyard, tripping our nuts off on acid. This graveyard was a common hangout spot for us in our acid-soaked youth. It meant we could avoid all the meat heads in the town centre getting violent after a few light ales. It had a wonderful vista over the town and there was also Greek's, our favourite fish and chip shop, at the bottom of a slope. Richard Trevithick, the pioneer of steam engines was also supposed to be buried in an unmarked grave there somewhere, so you would occasionally get some "steam buffs" turning up to honour the man, only to be confronted by a bunch of teenagers out of their heads on LSD.

During this day of us paying our psychedelic respects to the dead, my old man Dave appeared out of nowhere and ran up to us sweating and shouting.

"Get yourself home. We've just been raided by the police."

It took me a while before I put two and two together.

Four rozzers had turned up at my parents' house and ransacked the place. They had been looking for a meth lab, only to find my parents sitting there, sipping tea, and watching the Saturday afternoon wrestling on TV. They weren't fans of the "sport", it was just the only thing that was remotely entertaining on the TV back in the days before satellite television.

Dave gave me a clip round the ear and dragged me home. Once there, I told my parents I was in no fit state to be taken to the pig shop and requested that they take me the following day. They both looked at me and realised I was well and truly out of my tiny little mind, so called the rozzers to tell them I would be turned in the following day. They then told me to go to bed. It was 6pm in the evening.

I spent the rest of the night smoking weed in my bedroom and lighting incense sticks to mask the smell of me smoking weed. My choice of music ranged from Boogie Down Productions, Public Enemy, Baaba Maal, Cat Stevens and early-period Genesis. My choice of visuals ranged from the intrinsic detail of the lines on my fingers and palms of my hands and the technicoloured kaleidoscope of faces that magically adorned the ceiling of my room.

Morning came. I had a spliff, then made my way to the kitchen for a pint of concentrated orange juice and a couple of slices of toast. My parents were in the front room. I apologised to them both and told them that I would get myself ready for my visit to the police station. Dave told me he was going to walk there with me, as he wanted to make sure I went.

I went back to my room, rolled another spliff and had a think about how best to deal with the situation I now found myself in. I have always been a firm believer in inane gibber being the best form of attack, especially when it comes to potentially awkward situations. With this in mind, I decided to put some photos from my recent holiday to Cornwall in my bag just in case the opportunity arose to showcase these to the unsuspecting police officers.

On the walk to the police station, Dave constantly reminded me that he and my mother were bitterly disappointed in me and that I was throwing my life away. I just let him have his say and didn't respond.

We arrived at the police station and informed the rozzer at the desk who we were, then waited in the reception area to be called. After approximately 15 minutes of sitting in silence, two police officers came out and beckoned for me to follow them. The rozzers told Dave that he was not required, and they only wanted to speak to me. Looking mildly panicked at this, Dave blurted out, "He's a good lad. I know he's been stupid, but he's a good lad. He likes a drink, and he likes to have a dabble now and then, but he wouldn't hurt a fly."

The rozzers looked at him and said nothing.

"You. Follow us."

I turned to Dave. "Don't worry. Go home. I'll catch you later."

I was led to the same interview room that I had frequented the previous week and was asked to explain why they found my train pass with a couple of acid tabs in the back of their van. I told them that it must have fallen out of my pocket by mistake, and that I was wondering where that was, as I needed my train pass to get to work on the Monday. They both frowned and centred their questioning around the LSD and not my difficulties at getting to the office on the previous Monday morning. I insisted that I wasn't a big-time drug dealer and that I had bought the acid off some surfer dude whilst I was on holiday in Cornwall. I told them that I couldn't remember what he looked like and now realise what a hideous mistake it all was. The rozzers just looked at me in silent disbelief. I then remembered the photos.

"It's true. I was in Cornwall. I have the photos in my bag if you want to look."

I took the photos out of my bag and proceeded to show them photos of seagulls, rock faces and general photos of me and my friends in varying states of inebriation. After a few minutes of flicking through my holiday snaps, the two police officers stood up.

"You can leave."

"What?"

"We said you can leave."

"You're not going to arrest me?"

"No."

"Can I have my train pass back?"

"Get out."

I was ushered out of the interview room and out the front door. I didn't look back, but I heard it slam firmly behind me.

I decided to go straight to the graveyard to tell the lads the good news and explain what had happened. They passed me a spliff, which I promptly lit. They then passed me an acid tab. I stuck it in my mouth. Then we spent the rest of the day looking meticulously at our fingers and palms of our hands. Seeing as it was a celebration, we even decided to check out a few blades of grass, twigs and leaves too.

Smoke on the water

18.
OPIUM KIDNAP

Luang Prabang, Laos. 2003.

I went to Luang Prabang to check out why UNE-SCO decided to allocate the whole town the honour of being a World Heritage Site. The hotel I was staying at was based in the idyllic paddy fields surrounding the town, so I took the shuttle bus down to the centre. I was dropped off and started walking towards the first of what I was assuming to be numerous Buddhist temples on my itinerary that late afternoon. I walked past a local, who was loitering in a side street that led down to the Mekong River.

"Hey, mister. You want opium?" he asked me kindly.

I laughed, nervously.

"No. I go temple."

A few minutes later, I arrived at a temple and walked through the gates. I entered a beautifully ornate, cobbled courtyard. In the centre of the courtyard were two pillared buildings, each with gold-leaf-encrusted walls, which contained colourful, intrinsic artwork and carvings. I could hear the drums and hums from Buddhist monks reciting their mantras as they meditated. I stood there motionless, taking in the beautiful sight and atmosphere for as long as my mind let me before getting distracted. I then thought of the man I had encountered on my walk here.

Fuck this shit. I'm going to try some opium.

I'd never smoked opium before, though I'd enjoyed (wrong word, but you know what I mean) a six-month heroin stint, before moving to Hong Kong. I loved the warm, encompassing tranquility of heroin, so thought opium was well worth a look-see (think 50 spliffs of premium indica skunk weed – that's heroin).

I turned around, strutted out the gate and went to try and find my new best friend. I eventually found him, chilling next to his boat on the banks of the Mekong River.

"Can I have some of your opium please?"

"Yes. You come on my boat. Smoke opium, then I take you to my family for dinner."

"Er, no, mate," I replied. "Can I just have some opium to take-away… back to my hotel?"

"No, sir. You come to my house for dinner. I take you back to hotel on my bike. My house is far."

"No, mate. I do not go to your house. I go hotel."

"Yes, sir. Come with me."

Thinking that we had sorted all of that out, I agreed to clamber into a tiny little cabin on his long, thin, wooden boat.

The cabin on his boat was dark. He lit a candle, then shuffled over to a box and rummaged around until he found a chillum, a lighter and a lump of opium. He broke off a bit of the opium and stuffed it into one end of the chillum. He then handed me the chillum and the lighter.

"You smoke now."

I smoked and instantly relaxed into a hazy, niceness. Once I'd finished chugging through the first lump, he instantly put another lump of opium in the chillum.

"You smoke now."

"You don't smoke?" I enquired.

"No. No, smoke. You smoke now."

"OK. How much does this cost, anyway?"

"1 dollar, one smoke."

Feeling this was a bargain, I just couldn't refuse. I eagerly lit the chillum, took a deep breath, and exhaled. The room was now starting to fill with a lovely scent. I relaxed a bit more. Another lump, another smoke, another dollar, another lump, another smoke, another dollar, another lump, another smoke, another dollar.

Pretty soon, I was out of my head. I then asked him whether

he could get hold of some ganja.

"Yes. How much you want?"

"I don't know. About 5 dollars' worth?"

"OK. I get ganja, then go to my house."

"No..."

He stood up, left the cabin, and started the engine of the boat.

"Oh, for fuck's sake!"

He shouted through the door. "My house on other side of river."

And with that, we motored across the Mekong, on my way to Kidnapville. I could barely remember my own name by this point, so I decided to stay in the cabin for a few minutes, so that I could get my head together and think what I should do with myself in this predicament. I decided that I had no other choice but to go with the flow, so stood up and stumbled out of the small cabin, to join him at the back of the boat. As soon as I left the cabin, he started slowing down. It was now pitch-black outside. I could make out some small lights in the distance, but apart from that, it was total heart of darkness. The boat now slowed to a crawl. I could just about make out another few wooden boats moored up on the riverbank. We banged into the sides of a couple, as we slowly made our way to land, which did wonders for my balance. I had to grab the bloke's arm for support, so that I didn't crumple on to the floor. Soon, he stopped the engine, grabbed a rope and a torch, then jumped off the side of the boat and wrapped the rope around a wooden pole.

"Come. Come."

I couldn't see where the fuck I was going. I followed him and stumbled off the side of the boat, straight into ankle-deep water.

"My feet are fucking soaking, mon."

"Yes. Yes. You follow. Come. Come."

"But my feet are soaking wet."

'Yes. Yes. You come."

He then darted up the muddy riverbank, with his torch light. By the time I realised what was going on, he was a good 10 metres ahead of me, so I tripped and squelched my way out of the water and up the riverbank in almost complete darkness.

"Come. Come."

"Alright, mon. Hold on."

But he didn't hold on. He just scurried along, with his torch beaming in front of him. I struggled in vain with my left-foot-right-foot co-ordination and slowly watched, as his torch light disappeared into the distance. I was now in total darkness and could not see anything at all, apart from pitch-black. This led to pitch-black thoughts running through my mind, of my imminent death: me skewered on to a long pole by a laughing Laotian with a flashlight glued to his head. The only thing I thought I could do was to shout at the top of my voice.

"Oi!"

Ten seconds later, I could see a flashlight coming back towards me from the distance.

"Sorry, sir. Sorry, sir. Come. Come."

"Fucking hell, mon. Can you go a bit slower?"

"Come. Come."

He finally led me through a gap in a wooden fence, to a neighbourhood of wooden shacks on stilts. At least there was some light here. There didn't appear to be any electricity, though – every light appeared to be candle-powered.

"You have money? Ganja."

"What? Oh, right. Yeah. Hold on."

I gave him 5 dollars.

I waited outside as he went into one of the shacks. I soon noticed several small faces look out of the dimly lit shack he was in. I waved. They waved back with beaming smiles. He came running out after a couple of minutes with a plastic carrier bag full of weed. There must have been half a tree in there.

"How much is this?" I asked.

"5 dollar. You say f5 dollar."

"Fuck me. Cheers."

Bargain.

I stuffed the bag into my rucksack.

"Come. Come."

And off we went again. We meandered through the muddy alleyways that separated a number of these shacks, until he eventually beckoned me up the stairs of one.

"My house," he said.

I followed him. At the top of the stairs, I was greeted by his mother, father, and younger brother, all sitting on the wooden floor, eating food.

"Come. Come."

I took off my soaking-wet shoes and socks, then flopped on to the floor next to his younger brother. They were amazing. His mother handed me a plate and his father started piling loads of delicious, mildly spiced vegetable dishes on to it. None of them spoke a word of English, but the next hour and a half was spent eating fantastic food and being welcomed like a long-lost son into this stranger's family.

Whenever I go on a trip, I always try to bring a few small bits and pieces to hand out to locals as gifts. I remembered I had some toy cars in my bag. After finishing my food, I picked one of the cars out of my bag and gave it to the man's younger brother. I had never seen such a beam of happiness emanate from a child's face before. He immediately stood up and rushed outside. Within a minute, he came pelting back through the door with the toy car and a gigantic, mutant cockroach, the size of a clenched fist, perched on the top of it.

For the next five minutes, I watched as the cockroach was sped around the room on top of this toy car. His little brother noticed the enjoyment I was getting from watching him and offered up the cockroach-car combo to me.

"Er, no thanks. You keep."

Worried that I was going to be forced to play with the cockroach, I looked at my man and told him that maybe it was time to leave.

After some big hugs with his mum, dad, brother, and cockroach, I put my still soaked-shoes and socks back on and was led to a motorbike. I jumped on the back, he revved up the engine, then took me on a crazy bike ride over cattle grids and through deep-ish streams. We arrived back at the hotel about 20 minutes later.

"Thanks, mate. You're a frickin' star," I told him.

We arranged to meet the following morning, so that he could take me out on his boat to some limestone cave with about 50,000 little Buddha statues inside. Back inside my hotel room, I locked the door and proceeded to plough my way through the tree in my bag.

I obviously didn't make it for the rendezvous the following day.

19.
TIT SICKNESS

I've never been into voluptuous ladies. Big breasts and a big booty have never really done it for me. If I can grab a nice little handful of titty or buttock I'm a happy man. I've also never been into blondes. I've always liked my ladies to be darker, both in hair colour and skin tone. The average Page 3 model just never did it for me when I was growing up. Sorry, Jakki.

It was the mid-nineties and I was living at the squat in Bethnal Green. I was bang out of my head on e-buzz (ecstasy) with Danger and Bon at the Scuzz House in London, when this buxom, blonde barmaid called Anna, invited me back to her house for a few spliffs. The lads were moving on to one of the many members' clubs we always managed to blag our way into –mainly by offering drugs to the doormen (or the celebrities that frequented these establishments) – but I wasn't really feeling up for a night of blathering away at people I didn't know. Anna lived in Covent Garden, so it was a convenient place to spend a few hours after closing time at the boozer. She was way out of my league, so I never ever thought that anything sexy would happen.

At closing time, the lads went on to the next joint and I waited for Anna to finish the last of her chores before we walked back to her flat. Before we left the boozer, we both downed a pill each (her first of the night and my fourth). Half an hour later, I could really feel the MDMA coursing through my veins. I was rushing big time and couldn't wait to get back to her pad for a big meaty spliff. When we arrived, I skinned up, whilst she made us both a vodka ginger ale and lime. She slipped on some acid jazz and we started gibbering nonsense on the sofa.

As we were chatting, I noticed that she rested her hand on my thigh, but didn't think anything of it, due to being out of our heads on e-buzz. Anna then started stroking my inner thigh.

Hello, I thought.

We shared another couple of spliffs, dropped another pill each and imbibed a few more vodkas. I was properly mullered, but not out of my head enough to be incoherent. Anna moved close to me, softly placed her finger over my lips and mouthed "shush". Thank fuck for that, I thought, I can't stop myself talking shit, so I'm pleased she's taken the initiative here and is doing it for me. She then leaned over and kissed me on my lips. A euphoric rush ran from my lips, through my body, straight to my cock. I kissed her back.

We sat on the sofa kissing and caressing each other through our clothes, careful not to touch any "sexual" areas, but close enough to drive the pleasure to a higher level. We both adjourned to her bedroom and soon the strokes of our hands began reaching each other's nether regions, which soon turned into the unbuttoning of shirts and trousers. She was sat on top of me, as I unbuttoned her shirt and undid her bra. I slipped both items of clothing off Anna, then out popped her melons. They were fucking massive. I knew they would be big, but now they were free of restrictive clothing, their full glory was revealed. Each one was bigger than my head. Straight away, I started thinking, *What the fuck am I supposed to do with these?*

I tried to put the size of her boobs to the back of my mind, which was obviously quite difficult, and just enjoy the experience of sharing love juices with another human being that you had deep feelings for. We both took the rest of our clothes off, and Anna started riding me. Her tits bounced up and down like enormous water-filled balloons. The sight started making me feel a little ill. I closed my eyes. The sight of these basketballs bouncing up and down started making me feel awkward and nauseated. They were too big to concentrate on anything else.

My mind started racing.

I tried to ride the discomfort out, but as we progressed in our love making, Anna leaned forward, arched her back and tried to position one of her nipples in my mouth, as she pushed my cock deeper inside her. *Shit, I think she wants me to suck her tits.*

I tried to kiss and lick her giant nipple as well as I could (with a conscious decision not to nibble at it, just in case she dug her nails into my body somewhere), but had to stop, as I had the fear I was going to be knocked unconscious by one of the fuckers; they swung like massive medicine balls. Proper fear.

I can picture them now, giant pendulums, bouncing up and down, side to side, defying gravity, and the thought of it still makes me queasy. Was it motion sickness? Was it the fear of being clocked in the face?

I wanted them to stop, but really didn't know how to achieve that. I could just stop and tell her to "stop swinging her fat tits around so much." I felt really bad – I didn't want to offend her, but couldn't think of the best way to finish off the job. I had stopped feeling pleasure and was now just feeling a mixture of guilt and queasiness.

Then an idea came to me. Not the best idea. But all I could come up with in that moment.

"Anna. I'm so sorry. I have to stop," I said. "I've got travel sickness."

Her face of joy quickly turned to disappointment. Then anger. A lot of anger.

"I'm really sorry," I said. "I can't do this anymore. I think your tits have given me motion sickness."

I shouldn't have said the last bit. But I was high as a lost balloon.

It was the last time she invited back to her flat. It was also the last time I ever dinked a woman with really big tits. Not for me. Sorry. But, then, I'm sure she felt the same about my big dick,right?

(DON'T DO) DRUGS

Welcome to the halfway stage of the chaos. To congratulate you on surviving this far – in much the same way as I have – I now feel obliged to give you the DRUGS WARN-ING, before it gets much worse. As you have discovered, most stories in my life reference my hedonistic youth and my excessive consumption of drugs and alcohol. Let me be clear: these references in no way mean that I encourage anyone to take drugs or drink booze to excess. Drugs do not agree with everyone, and I would always defer to caution, before advising anyone to just go mad for it, like I did. I have seen too many people die at an early age, or completely lose their marbles, including myself, to consider drug or alcohol abuse a harmless activity. Different people with alternative mindsets have mixed reactions to taking these mind-altering substances, and serious thought and research should be undertaken by everyone, prior to embarking on a drug and drink frenzy. And, remember, I had dumb fucking luck on my side.

I had a great tolerance of mistreating my body and mind. That said, I don't think I've come off it unscathed. I look about 50 years older than I am, and have dark bags under my eyes that sag down to my knees.

Oh, yes, I also have actual brain damage (more of this later)

Yes, if you should ever need any proof that drugs don't work, just take a look at my face. I've aged terribly.

I called this book *Dope* for a reason. This book is about dope shit I've done and some of that dope shit has been done while under the influence. Therefore, being true to myself and being true to you, the handsome reader, I need at least to be truthful.

Being tee-total now has brought me a greater reflection on my past. I am not ashamed of what I did, and in fact, I am extremely proud that I managed to live through what I did and come out the other end alive, with a slither of sanity left. It introduced me to aspects of life that I wouldn't have experienced if I had been a straight head all my life. And, thankfully, I didn't feel the need to become a born-again Christian, or monk, or meditation moron to see the light. The light found me – and it was good.

University College London Hospitals **NHS**
NHS Trust

GD/S ███████
NHS

The National Hospital for Neurology and Neurosurgery
Queen Square
London WC1N 3BG

Dictated: 12 May 2008
Typed: 14 May 2008

Telephone: 0845 155 5000 ext 72 3015
Fax: 020 7829 8784
Web-site: www.uclh.nhs.uk

MEDICAL IN CONFIDENCE

███████████

0208 447 3875

0844 477 8789

RE: ███████████████████

This gentleman's MRI brain revealed a T₂ waited hyperintensity in the left parietal white matter. This was within the watershed territory. There were a number of smaller lesions in the subcortical white matter within the left frontal lobe. There were also similar lesions in the subcortical white matter in the right superior frontal gyrus.
 — ? at edge of blood

The radiologists felt that the lesions were unusual and wondered about a vascular ischaemic aetiology. They also wondered perhaps about an inflammatory cause.

stroke

Of course, he presents with collapses which sound fairly typical for syncopal episodes. These first began when he was 13. He also has migraines. The collapses are now infrequent occurring every six months. He has also had an EEG which was normal.

I have phoned ███ today to let him know the results. *I have reassured him that the appearances are probably coincidental to his symptoms.* I asked him whether there was any history of birth trauma and he thought not. I note also a previous history of cocaine and heroin use but he has been off illicit drugs for the last six years.

The imaging appearances are likely to be very long-standing – possibly arising in the perinatal period. (I note that this is his first MRI – the imaging that he had as a teenager was actually a CT – not an MRI as mentioned in my first letter). The radiologists suggested further investigation with an intra and extracranial MRA, DWI, and a gadolinium enhanced MRI of his brain. I have arranged these and we will review him in the clinic with the results. *? this before his with abrupt*

Proof of my brain damage

20.
BRAIN DAMAGE

May 2008.

I was in the midst of discussing the nuances of accounting at a company I was courting, a client who specialised in investing in the development and management of medical centres, when I received a call on my mobile.

"Hello."

"Hello. Am I speaking to Wev?"

"Yes. How can I help you?"

"I am Dr Sheba, from the National Hospital for Neurology."

"Oh. Hello."

"I would like to inform you that we have received the test results from your MRI scan."

"OK…"

"Yes. Your MRI brain scan revealed a T2 weighted hyper-intensity in the left parietal white matter."

"That sounds wicked."

"Hmm… Quite… This was within the watershed territory."

"Was it? That's good news then, right?"

"There were a number of smaller lesions in the subcortical white matter within the left frontal lobe. There were also similar lesions in the subcortical white matter in the right superior frontal gyrus."

"The right superior frontal gyrus?"

"Yes. The radiologists felt that the lesions were unusual and wondered about a vascular ischaemic aetiology."

"Did they?"

"Yes, they did."

"And what do the radiologists recommend doing about the unusual lesions?"

"Well, they suggested further investigation with an intra and extracranial MRA, DWI, and gadolinium-enhanced MRI of your brain."

"Wicked. Well, at least that's all sorted then. I'm sorry, doctor, but I'm busy at work. Is that all?"

"Er, well, apart from arranging an appointment for your intra- and extracranial MRA, DWI, and gadolinium-enhanced MRI of your brain, yes, I suppose it is."

"Excellent. I'm in Chester at the moment, so can we arrange one for next week, when I'm back in London?"

"Er, I think we need to get you to London sooner than next week. Do you understand what I've just said to you?"

"To be quite honest, doctor, you lost me at 'Hello'."

"I thought so."

There was an *X-Factor* style pause in the conversation, which made me think I was about to go through to the next round of the competition.

"You've got brain damage."

Or, maybe not.

"What?"

"Sorry to have to be the one to tell you, but…"

"Err… hold on a second, doctor."

I turned to my client.

"Sorry, mon. I have to take this call."

They all nodded in unison.

I stood up and left the office and made my way outside. I rolled up a cigarette and sat on the grass as the doctor explained everything again, only this time a lot slower, which was apt, because he told me I had brain damage. I went back to the office to explain to the client that I had to terminate the meeting due to some personal news, and had to return to London immediately for more tests. My face must have been a sight to see.

"Wev, are you alright?"

"Not really."

"Oh dear. What's wrong?"

"I've just been told I've got (I also left an *X-Factor* style pause here just to heighten the drama)... brain... damage."

And with that, off I trotted back to London for six months of brain tests.

The doctors never found the root cause for the brain damage, but I assumed it was a lifetime of hard drugs, booze, and treating my body with little respect. Somewhat stupidly, I didn't give up the hard drugs and booze – not immediately.

Blame the brain damage.

Stoned at the top of Glastonbury Tor

21.
CRACKHEAD HEADBUTT

As mentioned in the introduction, my cheery disposition has led me to approach strangers and greet them with a cheesy grin and a salutation. I tend to get away with it when I am abroad – what can I say, I'm charming – but approaching an unknown entity in the UK and saying hello can often lead to – at the very least – strange looks, and at most (in my case anyway) a headbutt. I can't understand why Brits are so averse – almost petrified – of saying hello to one another. It's a nice thing to do, right? It always brings a smile to my face. In fact, it's this ability to approach anyone and everyone that has made my life a happy one and opened up many opportunities to partake in dumb shit.

The first, and only, time I was headbutted was in late 1999. I was visiting Keels in Shrewsbury. He was back in the UK on a visit from Colombia. It was a Saturday. We were walking up the busy high street, and as usual, I was exchanging pleasantries with the local populace. As always, everyone ignored me.

Except one guy. A crackhead. Of that, I am sure.

"Alright there, mon?" I said to him, as I walked down the street.

He looked at me, shot me an angry look and then charged at me.

Before I could even understand what the fuck was going on, he jumped up, and headbutted me clean on my forehead.

I fell down in the same way a potato would if it had been headbutted. I immediately tasted blood, and assumed it was mine. I was right.

As my ears filled up with blood, all I could hear was "Get up, you fucking fag!"

I obviously stood up, thanks to Keels, and ran away as fast as I could. The crackhead ran after us! He was shouting and screaming obscenities, as if I'd just fucked his mother. I really couldn't understand it. I pushed myself past a couple of women and children, but he was catching up with me. I honestly thought he was going to beat the living shit out of me just for saying hello, so decided that rather than deal with this in the street, that I should run into a shop. We ducked into the first one we could – a pharmacy.

I ran straight through the doors and stood in an aisle, panting, blood leaking out and down my face. My nose felt flattened. My ears were ringing. My head killed.

The crackhead stopped at the entrance and started shouting, "Come on out, you soft Southern wanker."

I shouted "No!" thinking that might scare him off.

The pharmacy customers were looking at me, shocked and scared that I was going to go on some sort of violent rampage. I turned to an elderly couple and explained to them that I only said hello to the lunatic outside and now he wanted to kill me. The old lady asked, "Where are you from, love?"

I replied "London". She looked at me with hostility. "Oh."

Immediately, I realised that maybe my loud, booming estuary English accent is probably not welcome in this part of the country. I looked back out the entrance. The crackhead was still doing his nut. Jumping up and down, shouting and swearing about how he was "going to rip my nutsack off".

I didn't know what to do, but I did know that I should hide myself out of sight from the crazed drug addict. I walked to the far end of the aisle and turned left, towards the shampoos and shower gels. Keels, who looked just as panicked as I was, spoke for the first time in a while.

"Fucking hell, Wev. Your face is... *mental*."

"Is it? Fuck. It does hurt a bit."

"Yeah. You look awful, like a sad, wet beetroot... Seeing as we're already in a chemist, why don't you buy some tissues, so you can wipe some of that blood off."

"Yeah. Maybe later, mon. I ain't leaving until that nutter outside stops shouting and screaming that he wants to kill me. Hopefully, he'll calm down in a minute."

Keels disappeared down an aisle. I spent the next couple of minutes pretending to look through shampoo brands on the shelves, and wipe blood somewhere less obvious than my face. I spotted a papaya extract one that I recognised from somewhere but couldn't remember where. Keels then returned with a packet of tissues and told me that he had already paid for them and to get wiping.

"The crackhead looks as if he's calmed down a little bit."

"What is he doing?"

"He's just leaning on the window, smoking a cigarette. He's not leaving 'cos he's not got much else to do, I guess."

"Oh, great, I'm going to die just because he's bored."

We waited another five minutes, then Keels checked again. The crackhead had gone.

"Thank fuck for that," I said as I tried to sop up the blood leaking from my sizeable head wound.* We crept very slowly to the counter, then very quickly out of the entrance and down the street.

What did I learn from all this? Leave Shrewsbury alone.

[*FYI, my face looked a lot worse than it actually seemed. A lot of bruising under my eyes, a large cut on my forehead and a bent-out-of-shape nose (and ego), but nothing a few spliffs in bed wouldn't fix.]

High as a kite

22.
ALMOST MARRIED

Whilst playing my daily volleyball game with the locals in Wayasewa Island, Fiji, circa 2004, it was difficult not to notice that a lot of them had some sort of deformity. However, it appeared to me that each and every one of them, owned their disability proudly and used it to their advantage. There were a number of volleyball players who had seriously disfigured hands and wrists, literal little red stubs at between 90 to 125-degree angles to their arms. Some of them didn't have forearms and had these red stubs at the same angle to their elbows. These were serious weapons when it came to the game of volleyball, as they could hammer the ball into the opposing court with a power that a normal hand/wrist combination would not be able to achieve.

Whilst enjoying watching the game and a drink with the chief's son at my resort's bar, he informed me that the islands ,population of 450 is descended from only three families. This astounded me, but on reflection now made complete sense as to why there were so many deformities in the local population. There must have been a great deal of inbreeding going on down on the island, to keep the population going. I had never considered it before, but if you live on a tiny island in the middle of the Pacific, the only way to stop your family bloodline from dying out is to fuck your cousins.

As I was not related to anyone on the island, I felt absolutely fine in telling the chief's son that one of the hotel's staff – a woman – was an absolute beauty. Just wow. She had long, flowing brown hair and a creamy dark skin. Think Thandiwe Newton, and you're halfway there. I told the chief's son that she was a stunner.

"That is Lani," he said.

"Well, Lani is lovely."

"I can arrange for you. She will be happy for you to be husband."

"What?"

The situation had escalated quickly.

"She is good woman. Very strong."

We carried on drinking and after a while I forgot about this little discussion.

The next morning, I decided to take advantage of the massage that was on offer at the resort. The staff at reception told me to wait in my little hut and that the masseur will be with me shortly.

Moments later, low and behold, Lani appeared in the doorway, ready to give me a massage.

The memories of the previous day's conversation came flooding back into my mind.

As I lay on bed face down, I was positive that the chief's son held enough influence and power at the resort to ensure Lani was the staff member to give me a massage, in the hope that we'd get it together, so that there could soon be a lovely new strain of mad-cow-disease infested, English blood flowing through their community.

Suddenly, I was lost for words.

I had been pimped out. To go ahead with the massage would be basically akin to asking Lani to marry me.

While the marriage proposal scared me, I was keen to see what Lani's massage skills were like. I'm a curious man, after all.

Lani asked me to take my top off, which I happily did, and she gently positioned me into place. She placed a tub of what looked like pig fat on my bedside table, scooped up a handful, slathered it over my back and sensually began to work on the knots down my spine. I soon started easing into a meditative bliss. There was very little conversation, but plenty of squelchy noises. I started to have thoughts that maybe a life with Lani on Wayasewa Island could be a wonderful way of living the rest of my days. She soon woke me out of my blissful splendour. "You like me for wife?" she whispered.

I sat up. And thought about her proposal for a minute. It wasn't the happy ending I was hoping for.

I then spent the next five minutes explaining to her that, as beautiful as she was, it was not customary in England to marry the masseur you'd only just met. I put my clothes back on and left a dejected Lani to her lard. I didn't feel sorry for her –as if she had seen my hairy arse, she would have backtracked on the proposal almost immediately anyway.

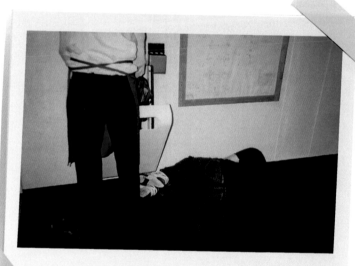

Asleep on a ferry

23.
NEW BROTHER

I was in my early thirties, living in Hong Kong and developing a mid-life crisis when I decided it was time to try to find out more about my biological father. I never saw him or heard from him since we moved down to the outskirts of London from Liverpool when I was a slobbering one-year-old. I knew he had died at some point when I was a teenager, so there was no way I was going to meet the man, but my two sisters and I, Woo and Moo, felt we needed some sort of closure. So, we decided to meet up with whatever family we had from the paternal side of our bloodline.

I gathered as much genealogical information as I could (only to later find that most of it was misinformation). In the end, I paid for an advert in the *Liverpool Echo* newspaper.

Within one week of the advert being printed, I was contacted by a cousin, Swirly. She told me that I had a brother, called Ian, and a lot of people who desperately wanted to meet my sisters and me. Within two weeks, I was on a flight back to the UK, so that we could meet our father's family.

We had only spoken to Swirly a couple of times on the phone to arrange the visit, and nobody else. She had arranged a party with all the family at her house in West Derby on the Saturday at 2pm. We really didn't know what to expect, but she told us that she wasn't sure whether Ian would turn up to the party. Us getting in touch had freaked Ian out quite a lot and due to him still being a bit fucked up from the death of his/our father, he didn't know whether seeing us would bring all that grief back, and was therefore non-committal on actually coming to the party.

Woo, Moo, and I kept our actual plan's secret from Lin and Dave due to the sensitivity of the situation. We lied and told them that we were going to a Beta Band gig together in Manchester.

When we arrived at Liverpool's finest Holiday Inn, we were all nervous as fuck. Naturally, I relied on my trusty herb to sedate my feelings. I caned quarter of an ounce of premium skunk to myself during the car journey up there. I felt great.

"Wev? Is that you?"

"Eh?" I looked up and saw a middle-aged Scouse woman standing over me.

"It's me – Swirly."

"Eh?" I couldn't comprehend what was happening. I was perhaps too stoned for the occasion.

"I'm your cousin, Swirly."

"Oh, shit. Hello, mon. You alright?"

Swirly then motioned to some geezer and an elderly lady, looking a tad apprehensive, a couple of feet behind her.

"This is your brother, Ian, and his mother, Eileen. We couldn't wait until tomorrow. We've been waiting here for your arrival as a surprise."

My sisters both burst out crying and ran over to Ian, and gave him large hugs. Ian burst out crying too. I sat on the ground in a daze.

"Fuck me," was the best I could muster as I shook my new brother's hand. "I have a brother... called... Ian," I said, effectively narrating the moment.

At the party the following day, we were each treated to a very unexpected and unusual gift. Woo and Moo each got a necklace, with some little heart thang and I was handed a small piece of folded-up tin foil. "Sorry, Wev. We just didn't know what to get you. We thought you all might appreciate some of your dad's ashes, so girls, you've both got some inside those hearts and Wev, yours is in the tin foil."

"Er, thanks," I said.

While, I made it back to the Holiday Inn that night, the tin foil didn't.

24.
TARANTULA

While on the "Dead Man Walking Tour" of South America, Keels and I camped out in the Amazon jungle. One night, on the edge of sleep, I was jolted upright by the sight of a large shadow on the outside of our tent. The shadow was the size of a football.

I opened my eyes.

"Fucking hell!" I yelled.

Keels woke up. I pointed to the shadow. He turned on his torch.

There was a tarantula approximately one foot above my head on the outside of the tent canvas.

"Shit, Keels. It's fucking moving."

The tarantula slowly moved around the outside of our tent.

This exact moment was the most terrified I have ever been. More than any other situation I have ever been in my life. I feared, genuinely, that this massive hairy spider was about to eat me and my friend whole. *Why else was it there?*

Keels took control of the situation and calmed me down.

We, very slowly, crept out of the tent, careful not to disturb the tarantula.

Raymond, our guide, was still awake and had noticed the tarantula on our tent. He told us not to worry. Raymond, then went to the tent to take a look. It was still there.

"Is it poisonous, Raymond?" I yelped.

"No. No poison," Raymond said – rather unconvincingly, I must say.

Desperate to not have two scared Brits sleep in his tent,

Raymond decided to scare the spider off. He scavenged around the ground and found four long sticks. He handed me and Keels a stick each and told us to prod it, to try to get it off the tent.

With our flashlights on, we prodded and prodded. It didn't budge. We all then started prodding at it again. It was a strong old fucker, as no matter how much we prodded, it held its ground. Seeing as we were getting nowhere fast, Raymond suggested that we all hold a corner of the tent and throw it in the air.

"Throw in air. Run," he said.

"Run? Why run? Spider no poison, right?"

He laughed.

"Oh, nice one, Raymond. I thought you said the tarantula wasn't poisonous?"

He laughed.

So, Keels, Raymond, and I each held a corner of the tent each, while a big, old, fuck-off, non-poisonous tarantula bore its ugly fangs at us. On the count of three, we all threw the tent in the air and ran for our lives – about 20 metres or so. The tent crashed back down to the ground. We left it for a minute, picked up our sticks again, then edged closer to the tent. We couldn't see it. The tarantula had gone. Despite snuggling my stick, I didn't sleep a wink that night.

25.
BULLET BUS

I t was the end of the working week and the beginnings of another debauched weekend in London. I finished work in the city at 5.30 on the dot and jumped on the bus back to my pad in Camberwell, South London. I was now living on my own in a lovely little studio flat, in some swanky refurbished warehouse conversion, opposite a depressing tenement block. I'd had enough of living with Nelson, MJ, and The Mule, and was loving the freedom of living alone. I called my partner in grime, Danger.

"Is your brother coming out tonight?" I asked.

(Brother was our code for cocaine.)

"Yeah, man. A couple of my brothers are coming out. I've also got a gram of ket."

"Yeah. Nice one on the code there, Danger, you numpty. Hope the rozzers ain't listening."

"Oh yeah. Ha-ha."

I told Danger that I'd meet him down the Scuzz House in Soho at 9pm. We'd have a couple of drinks there and then move on to Fluffy's, a nearby boozer.

At 8pm, I left the house in a nicely sedated head state and stumbled down to the bus stop, with some nice Roots Reggae blasting away on my Sony Walkman.

Don't laugh, this was the mid-nineties, its all we had.

You can get a number of different buses from Camberwell Green to central London. Most of them go straight up the Walworth Road to Elephant and Castle, where you can then get the underground to the West End in 10 minutes. One bus, the P3, turns off the Walworth Road at Burgess Park and has a quick detour through one of the roughest estates in Europe (Google it): the Aylesbury Estate, and on to the Old Kent Road, which then leads you back to Elephant and Castle.

The P3 was the first bus to arrive, so I got on, and sat about two-thirds of the way down the bus and started to read my book, *My Traitor's Heart* by Rian Malan. There were only about two or three other passengers on the bus. I was in my own little world, listening to "Give Me" by Burning Spear and reading a bit in the book about when some poor fuckers in South Africa were burned alive in some car tyres.

Then, suddenly, a deafening noise – a deep thud – made me jump up from my seat. I stopped, looked up and saw the two passengers at the front of the bus staring at me – as if perhaps I was a ghost. It was startling to see how startled they were of me. They had supremely frightened expressions on their faces. I turned to my right and saw large cracks in the window next to me. I looked above me and saw what looked exactly like a bullet hole in the window, about two inches from my head.

I was speechless, except for "Shit."

I turned to my left and saw another bullet hole in the window on the other side of the bus, a couple of feet above the head of one of the other passengers. I took my earphones out.

"What the fuck just happened?"

"I don't know," one of the other passengers said, shocked, starting to shake. "I think someone is… shooting… *at the bus…* from the estate…"

"Shit."

The bus driver had obviously felt the impact of the bullets hit the bus and diverted off the route. As the bus turned a corner, both windows shattered. The one next to me showered me in hundreds of shards of glass. The glass that shattered from the other window smashed on to the road, shocking the shit out of me.

"Is everyone OK?" The bus driver pulled over and shouted at his passengers.

We all answered positively. He immediately phoned whomever you contact when these situations occur. He told us that the police would arrive shortly. We all waited in stunned silence for the next five minutes, before we heard the increasing sounds of sirens in the distance. As the sirens got nearer and nearer, they didn't slow down. A whole unit of police cars – maybe eight or so – sped right past the bus and then disappeared into the distance. We waited another couple of minutes in silence. After 10 minutes or so, a whole unit of police cars and vans turned up at the bus. A large crowd had gathered outside the bus too, looking at the passengers, wondering what we had done to deserve this, and inspecting the smashed glass.

When quizzed, I couldn't tell the police much about what happened, apart from the fact that before the glass smashed, two bullet holes appeared in the glass following a loud noise. I left my details and was told I could leave. And that was that.

During the nineties, the Aylesbury Estate was a no-go area for anyone that didn't live there (particularly the police), so I can only assume this shooting was brushed under the carpet, as one of those things that can happen on a Friday night in north Peckham. Nobody was killed or hurt, so the rozzers probably thought it was a bit of a dead end. Every time I listen to "Give Me" by Burning Spear, I am always transported back to that journey on the P3, and the sight of that bullet hole *just above my head.*

"I'm sure I will hold my head up straight on the line," indeed…

桂林观光纪念

Pictures of Guilin

Don't try this at home

26.
RIDE THE TIGER

While living in Hong Kong in 2005, my girlfriend, Kit Ling, and I booked ourselves on a tour group trip to Guilin, China. I've never been into tours and have only been on a couple as I prefer to see the world independently, but the price of the five-day tour was cheaper than any flight I could find on the internet. Obviously, being part of a tour group meant that we got dragged to restaurants and excursions that we would never have gone to and were not particularly interested in. One such place we had to visit was Guilin Zoo.

Guilin, and the surrounding area, is astoundingly beautiful. Hundreds of limestone karst hills stretching for miles along the River Li, massive caves within most of the hills, lush, green vegetation everywhere, and an abundance of beautiful lakes.

The zoo, however, was horrendous.

It was a grey concrete monstrosity. There was very little vegetation or grass and was the most unnatural setting you could house an animal. All the enclosures contained ill-looking animals, separated from the tourists by rusty metal bars. It was a dismal animal prison. We were disgusted.

Kit Ling and I were dragged through this place by our guide, along with another 20 Hong Kong Chinese who were on the tour with us. After an hour, we were getting very depressed.

We then came upon the tiger enclosure. Usually the highlight of any zoo tour. The Big Cat.

This tiger was massive. And it was contained in a circular cage that was no bigger than a boxing ring. As we circled around the cage, there was a big roar of excitement from the people at the front of our group. They all stopped and started chattering away in Mandarin with someone who I assumed was a zookeeper that looked after the tiger.

As we caught up with the front of the group, I noticed that the tiger's cage door was open. "What the fuck!" I exclaimed to Kit Ling, pointing and startled. With my loud, booming British voice bellowing across the zoo, everybody turned around and looked at me. This led to even more excited chatter, but this time, the excitement was predominantly coming from the zookeeper. He kept glancing at me and continued his animated discussion with four to five members of the tour group and the tour guide. The tour guide then beckoned Kit Ling over for a conversation. She left my side and went to find out what was going on. She glanced back at me a few times and laughed as the zookeeper and the tour guide gibbered something to her. They all laughed. I didn't have a clue what the frig was going on, as my Mandarin was a bit rusty.

After a minute or so, Kit Ling came walking back over to me. As she approached, I noticed that absolutely everyone in the vicinity followed her move and were now staring intensely at us both.

"What the fuck's going on?" I said.

"Er, yeah."

"What?"

"I don't really know how to say this."

"Say what?"

"Er, yeah."

"For fuck's sake, Kit Ling. Come on. Why is everyone staring at us?"

"Er, the zookeeper wants *you* to sit on the tiger...and ride it... like... a horse."

"What? The zookeeper wants me to sit on the frigging tiger?"

"Yes. And ride it. Like a horse."

"Well, the prick can just poke that idea right up his poo-pipe, can't he?"

"Wev, it's not that simple."

"What do you mean, it's not that simple? I ain't sitting on a fucking tiger."

"They told me that they might have to put the tiger down, if you don't sit on it?"

"What? What the fuck are you talking about?"

"Well, they told me that the zoo doesn't have any money, that is why all of the animals look so ill. The zookeeper said that if they don't start attracting more customers to the zoo soon, they will have to close the zoo and kill the animals as they can't afford to keep them."

"What? You're joking, ain't ya?"

"I'm not. That's what they told me."

"Well, that's pretty hideous, but I don't understand what that has to do with me sitting on a tiger."

"Yes. Well, one of the activities they want to offer, is for tourists to sit on a tiger. They want you to sit on the tiger and have your photo taken, so they could use it for their marketing."

My white face started to turn ever whiter.

"Why me?"

"You're a *gwailo* – the white devil."

"Come again?"

"They rarely get *gwailo* tourists visiting the zoo and the zoo-keeper said that a photo of a *gwailo* sitting on the tiger would attract more *gwailo* here than a photo of a Chinese person."

"I don't fucking believe this."

"If you don't sit on that tiger, and look like you're having fun, he said they'll have to shoot it."

"What if it eats me?"

"It won't. The zookeeper told me it is heavily drugged."

It did look stoned. I should know.

I shook my head in disbelief. "I can't believe this."

As I shook my head, there was a groan from the gathering crowd. If you've ever been the sole white person in a remote Asian village, you'll know that people will come for miles to see the *gwailo* out of its natural habitat.

I stood shaking for a few seconds. I ran through all the options: I obviously didn't want to sit on the tiger… but I didn't want it dead either. I looked into the eyes of the tiger, and saw just a miserable existence. If I could, in some small way, help to enhance its living conditions, and act as some sort of marketing tool – and I am a tool – then riding a tiger is the least I could do.

I looked at Kit Ling, then at the glum zookeeper. "Alright, I'll do it."

Once the zookeeper excitedly announced my involvement, the crowd erupted in rapture. Within minutes, the crowd tripled.

The zookeeper walked me to the open door and guided me around to the back of the tiger. The poor thing didn't even notice I was there. Nor did it care. With absolutely zero input from the zookeeper, I was simply asked to, "Ride the tiger… and smile!"

And so, being the performing *gwailo* that I am, I did just that.

There was a whir of clicks and flashes from the crowd and a thousand photos taken from the zookeeper. Since I committed to sitting on the tiger, and could see just how drugged it was, I surprisingly didn't have any fear, and was pretty relaxed as I sat on its back. I even began to stroke the top of its head and tickle it around the ears. The photo shoot finished after one minute, and the zookeeper told me I could leave the enclosure. He gave me two thumbs up as I walked out. At least he was happy.

The zookeeper turned to me and told me that the zoo would give me a photograph of me riding the tiger to show their appreciation of what I had done for the future of the zoo and the future wellbeing of the tiger.

My only regret was that I wasn't stoned myself.

27.
TOO MUCH VIAGRA

My work colleague, Teddy, was getting married to his girlfriend, Sarah, and he asked me to be his best man. I'd never been a best man before and was unsure what to do on the big night out. I decided to ask my weed dealer, Pillows, for local advice. He told me about Shep Hau, a little town in the Guangdong Province, China. There, according to Pillows, the bars were just full of women. They weren't prostitutes, per se, he said, but they were paid by the bars to flirt with and "entertain" any man that entered the establishment. Sounded like the ideal stag venue to me. Pillows also told me that he could also get hold of some Viagra for the occasion.

I mentioned the plan to Teddy, but he told me that he couldn't go, as if his wife-to-be ever found out, he'd be fucking shot. Fair play.

So, for Teddy's stag do, we left Teddy behind and went without him.

I booked a hotel for the night for Pillows and me and Pillows sorted out the Viagra. The plan was to get the 3pm train from Hung Hom train station to Guangzhou. Once there, it would take an hour-long taxi journey before we reached Shep Hau.

Pillows and I met up early at my apartment and smoked copious amounts of weed. We decided to take a little with us as immigration at Hung Hom train station was pretty lax.

We reached Shep Hau around 6pm and checked into our hotel. We had a couple of spliffs in my room, then Pillows pulled out the Viagra. We both downed one each, with a can of lager, then strutted down to the bars. The Viagra came up almost immediately, along with my penis. This was the first and only time I have ever taken Viagra and it felt a lot like when you come up on e-buzz; I started feeling lightheaded and my stomach started feeling sickly. The only difference was the massive hard-on that now stuck out of my shorts like a sore thumb. My stonk-on was obvious to anyone who was within a 5-mile radius. It felt as stiff as a crowbar. I felt a bit embarrassed by the whole affair, to be honest, but there wasn't much I could do about it, so I strutted into each bar, with my proud little brother tucked up under my belt and barely hidden by my untucked shirt.

When we walked in to the fourth or fifth bar, we were accosted by a couple of beautiful local girls. One of them pointed at my hard erect cock and started laughing. I laughed too... until she gave it an almighty flick with one of her fingers; it sent an intense shot of pain through my body. Pillows and I sat down in a booth, and two girls followed us. The next couple of hours were spent drinking, flirting, gibbering, and lightly petting the girls who came over.

The cheesy nineties dance tune, "Unbelievable" by EMF then suddenly came blasting through the speakers. The girl I was with asked me for a dance. Now being quite pissed, I couldn't refuse. She led me to the dance floor, where we had a bit of a smooch, with me grinding and thrusting my proud soldier at her belly button. She then pulled my shorts and pants down around my ankles and ran out of the bar laughing; she left me standing in the middle of the packed dance floor with my massive cock pointing upwards like an arrow. The rest of the dance floor laughed. I pulled my shorts back up and re-joined Pillows, who had been tossed aside like an oily rag by his woman. We both decided that we'd had enough of this and just went back to the hotel for a few smokes.

After sitting in the room with Pillows for 15 minutes, and with my cock pulsating like a mutant frog heart, I told Pillows that he needed to leave as it didn't sit comfortably with me to be so close to him whilst in such a condition. He left and I spent the next two hours, frapping away until I finally got the better of the Viagra and shot a load that almost hit the ceiling. Never again.

28.
TOO FUCKED TO FLY

I t was my last night in Laos and I still had a huge amount of weed to smoke.

"I can't just leave it here, and I can't take it with me," I said to myself in the mirror. "I'm just going to have to try and smoke it all… tonight."

I started chain-smoking bifters. By about 9pm, I realised that even if I smoked all night, I still wouldn't get through it all. Therefore, I decided to start eating it too. I had a puff on my spliff, then put my hand into the bag and pulled out a handful of twigs and scraped the bud off with my teeth. I'd then take a swig of English breakfast tea, have a bit of a swill and chew, to soften the weed up a bit and to ensure there weren't any sharp bits in there, then I'd swallow. This process was repeated time and again, until I realised that it was 3am in the morning and that I should go to sleep. I had a look at the damage and saw that there was only about a quarter of an ounce of weed left, so I rolled up a strong spliff to smoke in the morning before I checked out. Feeling immensely proud of myself for getting through such a large amount of herb, I fell into a deep, sedated sleep.

I woke at 8am and felt surprisingly well. I was a bit tired, but I didn't feel any weed hangover at all. I smoked the spliff I had saved and threw the twigs and remaining buds in the bin.

I was on my way to Siem Reap, Cambodia, but there were no direct flights from Luang Prabang, so I had to go via Bangkok. At the airport, I checked in for my flight to Bangkok, smoothly transitioned through immigration and made my way on to the plane. The plane was half-empty, so I was fortunate enough to have nobody sitting next to me and thought I could maybe catch up on a little sleep on the flight. The flight only lasted about an hour, but I estimated that I could get at least 30 minutes kip, which always helps after a late night. The plane taxied to the runway. Next, there was a rumble, as the plane's engines started revving up and off it sped, down the runway.

All of a sudden, I didn't feel so good.

"Shit. What the fuck's going on?"

My brain seemed to wake up – or switch off – as we sped along the runway. I literally didn't know what was happening as the plane launched itself into the sky.

"Shit. What the fuck's going on?"

As the plane ascended, higher and higher, my brain started to panic. As my body was being propelled into the clouds, so to was my head.

My vision started closing in on me. I gripped the arms of the seat 16C tightly; darkness started surrounding me until all I could see was a small speck of light at the end of a long, dark tunnel. The light started getting closer, then a little bit closer again, until the light opened into the cabin of the aeroplane.

"That's right. I'm on a friggin' plane," I whispered to myself.

I looked out of the window and could see the murky, brown Mekong River far below me, meandering through lush green jungle. Paranoid thoughts then started rushing through my head.

"What the fuck am I doing up here? This ain't natural," I whispered that out too loudly. Other passengers started to stare. I decided looking out the window was not good for my mental state, so tried looking around the cabin instead. I couldn't really focus on anything. I then realised that I was still clasping hold of the arms of my seat as if my life depended on it. I tried to let go, but my arms refused to release their grip. An air stewardess approached and mouthed something to me. I couldn't hear a word of what she said. She mouthed something again. I tried to mouth something back, but couldn't manage anything apart from a little dribble and a tightening of my clasp of the chair arms. She decided I was a lost cause and moved further down the cabin and out of my peripheral vision. The cacophony of sound in the cabin was a symphony of chaos in my head. Every sound was too loud, yet quiet, muffled yet sharp.

My heart was pulsing, my head was pounding. I could feel something in my brain moving around. Connections were firing but not received. I felt a pressure above my left eye, then it moved across my forehead, to my right ear, to the back of my head and then to my right eye. It was like a pinball pinging around my head.

"Shit. What the fuck is going on?"

This, and a whole lot else, continued for the duration of the flight.

Suddenly there was a big jolt forward as the plane juddered to a standstill at Bangkok airport. This hard landing sent my brain flying again. As soon as the "fasten seat belt" sign was not illuminated, I somehow found a way to get up from my seat, stumble off the plane and into the terminal. I felt everything.

"Right. Sort yourself out. What am I doing here?"

I couldn't remember where I was. Or where I was going. Or, rather dangerously, think of my own name in my mind.

"Wev," I said out loud. "Cambodia... I'm going to Cambodia."

I searched my pockets for my ticket and saw that my connecting flight was due to leave at 2.40pm. I managed to find a large departures monitor with a list of letters and numbers. I eventually worked out that the plane I needed was leaving from Gate 28 in 90 minutes.

"Gate 28. Gate 28. Where the fuck is Gate 28?"

I saw a geezer in a blue suit.

"Eight two gate," I slurred.

He smiled and vaguely pointed to somewhere in the far distance. Where that somewhere was, I did not know, but I just went in the direction he pointed. As I made my way through the terminal, I accidentally bumped into a lot of people, chairs and all the walls. I was unable to pay attention to what was immediately in front of me, or remember where I had come from, as I was too busy trying to comprehend every sign that came within sight, hoping for the magical Gate 28 lettering to appear.

And, after what seemed an eternity of sliding up and down airport walls, would you believe it: the gate magically appeared. I stood there, sweating, as I stared at the Gate 28 sign for a couple of minutes, then looked below the sign and noticed some stewardess woman looking nervously at me.

"Can I help you, sir?"

"Glate twent ate."

"I fumbled around and gave her my ticket. She looked at it, then looked at me with a rather sad expression.

"Sir. This is your ticket for the flight. Do you have the boarding pass?"

She stared deep into my optic spheres and saw only darkness.

"This is a ticket. I need your boarding pass."

"Tick it," I said.

"Yes, I know, but I need your boarding pass."

I stood there swaying from side to side.

"Sorry, sir, but I cannot let you on the plane without a boarding pass."

"But tick it," I said.

"I know, sir, but I need a boarding pass. Do you have a boarding pass?"

I nodded no.

"Sir. I understand you have a ticket, but I cannot let you on the plane without a boarding pass. Have you checked-in?"

"Laos," I murmured.

"Laos? You checked in at Laos? You are in Bangkok now. Did you check-in in Bangkok?"

"Whuh?"

"You need to check-in in Bangkok, otherwise you cannot get on this plane."

I just stood there.

My vision started playing tricks with me again and the tunnel of doom enveloped my sight. Each blink of my eyes felt as if it lasted an eternity. I saw things that were certainly not there.

"Sir. Do you need any help? I am sorry, but you cannot fly on this plane unless you have a boarding pass. We are closing the gate in 30 minutes. You have to hurry."

I stared at the Gate 28 sign and then stared at the stewardess. Sweat beads drooled down my balding swede. I let out a whimper. The stewardess stared at me, then picked up a walkie-talkie and started gibbering Thai down it.

"Sir, someone is coming to help you."

The next few minutes were spent with me standing in silence, sweating profusely, looking at the Gate 28 sign, then looking in desperation at the stewardess. The poor woman had no choice but to stay where she was and accept her fate, as other passengers were getting onboard and needed their boarding passes checked. After I don't know how long, another airline bloke in an airline suit came up to me.

"Sir. Can I help you?"

"What?"

A confused expression crossed his face. He looked at the stewardess. She spoke some Thai to him, then he turned back to me.

"Sir. You must follow me. I can help, but we have to be quick."

He started walking off. I stood there motionless. He turned around and noticed I hadn't moved an inch. He came back and grabbed me by the wrist.

"Sir. Come with me."

With a tug of my wrist, we were on our way. The man walking as fast as he could – me a sack of stoned potatoes on his hand, being dragged along like a deceased rat. He led me to a desk.

"Sir. I need your passport."

At this stage, I was well and truly lost. All I could muster was a grunt and a faint gesture towards my bag.

"Sir. Can I take the passport out of your bag?"

I looked at him and I think I smiled. He took this as authorisation that he could have a little delve through my bag and managed to find my passport in the front pocket. He handed it and my ticket to a woman behind the counter. Within a couple of minutes, the woman handed him back my passport and a shiny new boarding pass. He gave me a big grin.

"Hurry, sir. Your plane will leave soon."

He grabbed hold of my wrist again and dragged me back to Gate 28. He handed the boarding pass to the stewardess and the passport back to me.

"You can go on the flight now, sir."

"Whuh?"

"Please, sir. You can get on the plane."

A sense of relief overcame me.

I couldn't speak so simply put my hands together and did the praying motion. I must have looked mental.

The stewardess handed me the boarding pass and backed away behind the counter, so that she didn't have the same misfortune.

"Enjoy your flight," she chirped.

Once I was on the plane, and strapped in, I had the most miserable flight. It wasn't until I landed the other end that I started to regain control of who I was. And once I switched on again, like the seat belt sign, I felt an intense relief that I was the pilot of my own being.

That experience taught me that never, *ever*, should anyone – under any circumstance – munch an ounce of weed the night before flying. I had never had a delayed reaction like that before. The super-paranoid state that I went through still makes me shudder when I think of it today. It was perhaps the highest I have ever been on weed. And, trust me, you never want to have an out-of-body experience like that, especially when you're rushing to catch a flight in a foreign country.

29.
COCAINE BREAKFAST

After our compulsory breakfast of cocaine and coffee, while holidaying in the mountains surrounding Mérida, Venezuela, MJ and Kotch decided it would be a blast to go for a cycle ride while completely fucked. I thought this sounded like a terrible idea, but the boys wouldn't let me get out of it. Our other friend, Gyo, was allowed to stay behind for reasons I can't remember.

After having rented super-shitty bikes from a super-shitty local bike hire, the three of us made our way out of town and to the mountains. I kept on moaning, especially when we had to cycle up an incline. It was hard work. And I'd had a lot of coke for breakfast.

After our third incline and approximately 15 kilometres away from Mérida, I told the lads we needed to stop for a break of cocaine and spliff. MJ and Kotch happily agreed.

Even though it was hard work, the scenery was amazing. Jungle-clad mountains reaching up to the clouds and beyond. This part of the Andes contains the highest peaks in Venezuela that rise up to around 5,000 metres. It's proper beautiful. We wound our way along the sides of these mountains on well-tarmacked roads and stopped for our "picnics" at many of the waterfalls that we passed. I remember us even being stupid enough to climb up the side of one of these frigging waterfalls, forgetting that I had a knack for falling 30 feet to near death.

Time started getting on and we were approximately forty kilometres out of town, so decided it was time to start cycling back. We'd finished the last of the cocaine, so the energetic thrusts of momentum that pushed us up the steep inclines were a distant memory. There was one 2-kilometre rise that I just couldn't complete, so I shouted for the lads to wait at the top for me, as I got off the bike and pushed it up. My legs were fucked, I was sweating, and my energy levels were near zero.

Once I caught up with Kotch and MJ, they'd already rolled a spliff. We caned that and MJ suggested we commit to cycling back to town without stopping. I only agreed if we could have one more spliff before departing. The lads moaned, but rather than incur the wrath of Wev, they agreed to my request. By the time we were ready to start cycling again, the sky was turning from blue to orange, as the sun was bidding farewell to another day. There were no lights on these winding roads, but there were sheer drops of 3 to 500 feet on one side of the road and we had no lights on our bikes. We had to get back to town soon, otherwise it would have been too dangerous to carry on.

MJ and Kotch sped off down the side of the mountain, and I followed. I could see them stretching out further from me. However, I had the fear that if I went too fast, I would lose control and would cycle off the edge of the road and fall to my death, so I vigilantly kept applying pressure to the brakes to slow myself down, rather than just go with the flow. The descent was fantastic, though. It went on for miles. I lost sight of the lads, but just continued to enjoy the downhill ride, with the wind in my hair and the buzz from a day of weed and cocaine running through my body.

I soon came across a tight bend, with a waterfall crashing down on one side of the road and the water gushing across the road, to form another waterfall on the other side of the road, as it crashed down the side of the mountain. It looked amazing, but as I got closer, I became increasingly confused as to how I should navigate this little obstruction, out of my head and on two wheels at 40-kilometres per hour. I came to the bend where the waterfall came crashing down and as soon as the bike sped through the water that rushed across the road, I decided to apply the brakes.

That was a dumb-as-shit idea. As soon as I broke, the bike spun out on me. I literally did a 360-degree spin three times. My life flashed in front of me. Then I had an obscure vision of a typhoon and Hong Kong Harbour, as the 300-foot drop on the other side of the road rushed ever closer to me. I crashed in a heap on the road, at most 5-feet from falling to my death.

Properly shook up, I stood, shaking like a leaf. I checked myself over and didn't see much blood, apart from a few scrapes, where body had met tarmac. I had got off lightly. Conscious that the other lads were probably closing in on the outskirts of Mérida by now, I got back on the bike and edged my way down the side of the mountain until I reached the bottom and met up with the lads.

Obviously, they found my incident harrowing. As we handed the bikes back, I disembarked from mine and immediately fell in a heap on the floor. I couldn't fucking walk. My left ankle was just numb as fuck and I couldn't put any pressure on it. The lads picked me up and helped me back to the apartment. Gyo was sat there, eagerly anticipating my return. When he saw the state of me, and heard what happened, he proudly announced he had the cure and produced a big pile of cocaine, thrust a pile of it down my snozzer and then gave me a fat spliff laced with it too.

He was right. It was a cure of some sorts, as my whole body and mind became just as numb as my ankle. The problem was, I had to constantly take "the cure" for the next three days, until I was finally able to put pressure on my ankle and walk without using the lads as human crutches.

TOP 10: MOST DOPE

We interupt our regular programming to bring you the charts. Today's Top 10 is the 10 best – worst? – times I've most been off, and out of, my head.

After consultation with the drongoids, below is my best remembered guess at the times I was most fucked. They are not in any particular order, as it is very difficult to compare one against the other. None of these little titbits appear later in this book, but some may appear in Volume 2 if I can remember any more stories.

1. GLASTONBURY, 1998

(Crack, ketamine, ecstasy, cocaine, skunk, booze)

Danger and I were very conscious that the other 12 or so people we were camping with at Glastonbury were none too happy or impressed with our crack-taking escapades. It always made for awkward moments, if we discussed it or got crack paraphernalia out when these friends were about.

We were all sitting around a camp fire at our tents, after the night's music and partying had finished. Danger and I were desperate for some crack, so we "borrowed" one of our friends' chillums (who claimed it had been blessed by the Dalai Lama – sounds like obvious bullshit, that one) and quietly creeped into our tent. It took us five minutes of fumbling around in the dark before we had transferred a few sizeable chunks of crack into the chillum and sparked it up. We caned that, knocked up another one, then caned that too.

We left the tent and joined the others, who were still sitting around the campfire – a lot more pissed-off-looking than when I'd last seen them 15 minutes ago. Some went to bed, some turned their backs to us, but none of them spoke to us. They were all properly pissed off. It wasn't until Bon told us that we were lit up like a beacon and everyone could clearly see our silhouettes using the sacred smoking device as a crack pipe, that we sort of understood. Sort of…

2. SOLSBURY HILL, 1992
(Acid, skunk, booze)

Chief and I and a few others were at a protest about some dual carriage-way being built through this beautiful part of the world (we actually thought we were going to a festival). I was completely nutted on acid, took my shoes and socks off, then stupidly told everyone that if they stood up and walked away, I wouldn't know what to do.

They all stood up and walked off and I found myself waking up at around 7am the following morning… on my own… on the side of Solsbury Hill… with no shoes or socks on. I ran straight down the hill for 10 minutes until I stumbled upon a bungalow. I banged on the front door until some camp bloke in orange y-fronts answered. He laughed as I explained to him that I didn't know where the fuck I was or where the fuck I was going and that I didn't have any shoes or socks on.

He offered to drive me around to see whether I could find where Chief had parked his camper van. Somehow, we managed to find him. Luckily, I found him when I did, as the cunt was just about to drive back to London without me, so that he could go to the Criminal Justice Bill march, just to impress some fit Spanish women we were with.

3. SOHO, 2000
(Heroin, booze)

Danger and I were on a heroin and booze binge at a private members club. We popped to the bogs on a regular occurrence to chase the dragon, then went back to prop the bar and gibber shite to whichever unsuspecting minor celebrity was being gibbered shite to on that particular occasion.

The problem was, due to this being one of the first times we had taken heroin, we also couldn't stop puking up. We tried our best to keep it together, but soon realised that we were spending most of our time in the bogs, either smoking heroin or vomiting.

We decided to admit defeat just after midnight and spent the rest of the night back at the squat in Bethnal with a bucket each and some tin foil.

4. DARTFORD-SOHO, 2000

(Ecstasy, skunk, booze)

This particular session started with an all-nighter at Danger's mothers house in Dartford. Danger and I downed six bottles of red wine and four pills each, until, at 5am, we decided to have a coffee in Soho.

We got the first train up to London and had a coffee. We then remembered coffee was shit, so bought another bottle of wine. We drank that, downed another couple of pills and smoked a few spliffs in Soho Square. At around 8.30am we decided it was time to wake Bon up, who was living and working at MJ's boozer in Soho at the time.

MJ welcomed us both into his boozer with a pint each. We then stumbled up to Bon in bed, pulled at his legs until he woke up, and stuffed a pill in his mouth. The rest of the day was spent in MJ's boozer or the Scuzz House popping pills and drinking booze. The lads realised it was time to get me home, when I was looking out the window of the Scuzz telling the lads that Dartford was busy today and asking when Woo was coming round our house.

This particular session ended after I'd downed my eighteenth pill on the floor of my pad in Camberwell, fell asleep and proceeded to do hand movements that were previously only thought possible by Fijian volleyball players.

5. VENEZUELA, 2000
(Crack, cocaine, skunk)

My first-time taking crack was a ridiculous affair. I was on the "Dead Man Walking Tour" of South America and had previously befriended a couple of middle-aged reprobates called Horace and George in Mérida. Horace thought he was an alien. George had mechanical engineering qualifications up to his eyeballs, but told me that he was being kept "prisoner" by Horace's magical powers.

I bumped into Horace at a bus stop in town, and he used his magic to drag me back to the rancid room they were living in. George scored piles of coke and a few boulders of crack for about £2.50 (slight exaggeration there), then we spent the next five hours in their tiny room, in a dilapidated building with vermin, and insect, infested shared toilet and kitchen facilities with a few hundred other poor souls.

It was insanity, just non-stop smoking and snorting. It's true what they say about you never getting the same high as your first ever rock of crack. My head went places that day. I only decided that it was time to get out of there when Horace started telling me that he recognised messiah-like qualities in me. I got the fear that I was gonna get killed, stuffed and stuck on an altar in the corner of their room.

6. VENEZUELA, 2004
(Crack, cocaine, skunk)

It was the last 24 hours of the month-long stint that replaced Danger's heroin addiction with a heroin and crack addiction. Seeing as it was our last day/night, we decided to go for broke and see how far we could push our tolerance levels.

Fifty rocks each later, and after nearly blinding ourselves a few times with exploding lighters and makeshift crack pipes, we had run out. It was around 4am. We didn't have any money left, so decided to walk the 10 minutes to the local ATM, so that we could then pay a visit to the local dealer for more rocks.

On the way to the ATM, we were accosted by one of the local crack-heads, who decided to accompany us on our walk. Halfway through the journey, some rozzers confronted us, pushed us up against a wall and stuck a gun to our heads, demanding we hand over the drugs we had. We fortunately didn't have anything on us apart from my trusty Visa Electron debit card. We were going to the bank, to get some money, so that we could buy some drugs, but at this point in time, we were drug free. They gave us a thorough body search, including getting a good feel of our shrunken cock, and balls, but found nothing.

The crackhead told the rozzers to leave us alone, as we were with him. The panic that went through me and Danger with that little comment. Fuck that. We were not with him at all. We wished he'd just fuck off, as he is no doubt the reason the rozzers are currently groping us both, with a gun to our heads. They let us go and told us to just get back to our hotel, which we did, after telling the crackhead to fuck off, withdrawing a load of cash and visiting the dealer for another 20 rocks each.

7. HONG KONG, 2006
(Booze)

I was on a session with two high-fliers. After downing a few Long Island Iced Teas and a bottle of expensive whiskey, I stumbled into a cabinet at the bar we were in, and knocked all of the establishment's crockery on the floor, where it proceeded to smash into thousands of tiny little pieces. Fortunately, these two high-fliers, were also very rich high-fliers, and paid the hefty bill for my minor misdemeanour.

After paying the proprietor off, they decided to take me to some swanky karaoke bar to meet some of their friends. After a couple of impressions of Mick Jagger and a few more whiskeys, I was convinced that these "friends" were in fact major players on the local Triad scene, as there was a constant flow of dangerous-looking, tattooed men coming in, getting some instructions and then trotting off again. There were also countless beautiful girls who were at the beck and call of these men.

Having a fair old amount of booze courage, I decided to confront them with a classic "Come on, mons. You're fucking Triads. Just admit it." They weren't having any of it, but I just kept repeating it over and over.

It wasn't until one of my high-flier mates was given a little whisper in the ear, that I was carted out of the place. I think they saved my life that particular night. However, I never got a chance to thank them for this, as they immediately stopped answering my calls.

8. HONG KONG, 2002
(Booze)

The dentist chair. What more do I have to say? It was around 1am and a bunch of us were at some nightclub in Admiralty Hong Kong, when someone suggested doing the "Dentist Chair" (made famous by Gazza during Euro 96).

I managed to last for the duration of the constant stream of vodka being poured down my gullet, but any proudness of this feat was quickly replaced with regret, as my night ended on a sour note. I thought it would be hilarious if I booted my boss down an escalator that took us down to the street for our respective taxis home. He flew down the escalator head first, but fortunately didn't land straight on his face, so got away with a couple of stitches in his knee and an expensively blood-stained suit. Could have been worse...

9. SOHO, 2000
(Heroin, Valium, cocaine, skunk, booze)

Danger and I were bang out of our heads. It was 1pm and we were in the Scuzz House, sipping away at our first vodka ginger beers of the day. We were a total mash-up. At best, our heads were in our hands. At worst, our heads were resting on the table in front of us, with dribble emanating from our noses and mouths.

We'd woken up that morning and realised we'd run out of coke, so washed down the last of the brown and Valiums we had, with an extremely healthy dosage of skunk weed. We organised meeting our coke dealer at his office around 3pm, so decided to have a couple of beverages down the Scuzz, before meeting him. It wasn't until we reached the Scuzz, that we realised we couldn't really focus on anything and were as sedated as a Chinese tiger.

We somehow managed to drag ourselves from the Scuzz House to the dealer's office. We had two fat lines each, then the gibber started. When we were back at the Scuzz House, we were the life and soul of the party. Non-stop banter for the next six hours. Fucking idiots.

10. BETHNAL GREEN, 1999
(Skunk tea, skunk)

Pretty much every night spent at the squat in Bethnal Green, was spent with a hash tea and a jamming session in the studio that the lads had set up in the basement downstairs. Over the months, our tolerance to hash tea had increased to the point, where we each had about a quarter of an ounce of your finest Moroccan in our respective cups. As the tolerance levels increased, the love of progressively, abstract sounds emanating from our resident house band, "Bundy" increased.

I had a particular love for the "Jen" keyboard, a funky, seventies number with loads of special effects. It also meant you could get away with having much musical talent, but still remain part of the collective, group sound in a positive way. Well, that was, apart from on this night.

I was too busy being taken tos some incredibly amazing places in my mind, while thinking I was blasting out a two-minute keyboard solo, to realise that, all of my friends were pointing at me, laughing, as my face lay down on the keyboard, and my nose played a pretty horrific C-minor.

"

THE MORE STUPID ONE IS,
THE CLOSER ONE IS TO REALITY.

THE MORE STUPID ONE IS,
THE CLEARER ONE IS.

STUPIDITY IS BRIEF AND ARTLESS,
WHILE INTELLIGENCE SQUIRMS
AND HIDES ITSELF.

INTELLIGENCE IS UNPRINCIPLED,
BUT STUPIDITY IS HONEST.
AND STRAIGHTFORWARD.

"

FYODOR DOSTOEVSKY

30.
THE SUIT

During my years of living at a squat in Bethnal Green, I, rather paradoxically, worked in a skyscraper in the City of London. One day, everyone in the office was extremely nervous as there was an anti-capitalist march planned for that day and the protestors were due to stomp past our office en route to the Bank of England. Rumours were swirling that some violent anarchists were going to go on a window-smashing rampage and potentially attack any wanker wearing a suit. Which was everyone in that part of London. Not much work was done that morning due to the fear factor kicking in amongst my colleagues. I, however, was not nervous at all, as I was due to meet a group of about 10 of my friends from Dartford at lunchtime, so that we could all go to the protest together.

At 11.45am, I got a phone call from one of our lovely receptionists sounding a little scared. She told me that one of my friends was waiting for me in reception. I told my boss I was popping out for lunch. Everyone in the office gasped. "What? You're going outside? Are you mental? There are anarchists outside. You'll get yourself killed!" I shrugged as I put my suit jacket on. When I reached reception, I saw the receptionist cowering behind her desk and looking terrified. Chief, who looked the antithesis of a suit, was sitting on one of the pristine chairs with a swarm of flies hovering over his greasy, long hair. I told him to get out the chair and leave, as he was scaring the poor young lady. He stood up and followed me out, leaving a dark, oily stain on the chair.

We both walked out the front door to meet the rest of the

lads. True to form, they were loitering and smoking weed. One of them handed me a spliff and off we went to the march. It only took a couple of minutes before we were all in the main throng of the protest.

Protests are wicked. They are like mini impromptu festivals. There were sound systems blaring, people dancing, and a whole heap of ganja being passed around.

Normally I don't mind people staring at me, confused. But on this particular day, I really did stand out like a sore thumb. I realised I was the only fucker at the anti-capitalist protest wearing an expensive Italian suit. This sort of thing has never really bothered me, as it had been a constant throughout my late teens and early twenties; I had been known on numerous occasions to meet the boys immediately after work and pop along to punk gigs, still in a work suit.

The protest – thousands of people all forming a disorderly queue – started moving slowly from Liverpool Street station along London Wall. The police obviously didn't want the protestors to take this particular route – lots of financial institutions to get angry at – as there were scores of riot police units lining the road. Sensing that this could antagonise the crowd, they backed away and were replaced by four meat wagons that sat parked next to each other in the street. I'm not really sure how the police thought this would stop the thousands of people descending upon them, as the police vans were soon surrounded by a bunch of pissed and stoned protestors, pelting eggs at them. While the atmosphere was eggy, that was all. Everyone in the crowd was in high spirits, enjoying the sun, enjoying the music, enjoying the ganja and enjoying the freedom a protest gives you to throw fresh dairy at the local constabulary.

The lads and I had a good view of all this mayhem as we stood on a wall at the side of the street constantly passing spliffs and cans of lager between each other. My mind started wandering as I thought about all these eggs being thrown at the police vans, impressed at the pre-planning that the protestors had put into their choice of missile to throw at the police. I turned to Chief.

"Where the fuck did all of these eggs come from?"

"What do you mean?"

"Well, who in their right mind carries a load of eggs with them to a protest?"

"Why? You got a problem with it?"

"No. I just don't understand why so many people have brought eggs with them."

"To throw at the fucking police you idiot."

"Oh, right…"

Chief then let out a sneaky little chuckle, opened his backpack and proudly pulled out two dozen free-range eggs.

"I popped into Sainsbury's before we met you."

"Free range? Let's hope they're long range!" I quipped.

I cracked up laughing, as he handed each of us two eggs each. We all threw our eggs in the direction of the police vans. Most of our eggs missed the meat wagons and smashed on the ground. One of mine splattered against the back of a protestor, who turned around sharply, confused about where it came from. I grimaced; I was concerned there was about to be a suit bashing, but he soon turned around again and continued hurling abuse at the rozzers.

The police must have got a call to get the fuck out of there – the sirens on the police vans suddenly started wailing and three of the vans slowly edged their way out of the crowd and back behind the police lines. The fourth van, however, reversed 10 metres, and shunted into a set of traffic lights, knocking them over. Everyone started cracking up laughing, and decided to pelt the van with more eggs, then a couple of protestors jumped on to the roof of the van and started doing some techno mental, mental dance.

The sirens of the police van started up again, and it jolted forward. This threw the two people on its roof, off balance. They quickly jumped down. Then the police van sped out of the crowds, and in the process, ran over a couple of protestors who couldn't get out of the way in time. It made me feel sick, as I saw the panic in the people's faces, then the bump of the van, as the wheels ran them over, as they fell to the floor.

Instantly, the protest turned from a party like vibe to really moody. There was anger and panic, as people rushed to the injured protestors to see how they were – then out of nowhere, the eggs were soon replaced with bricks, and shop windows started getting smashed. I again wondered at how prepared the protestors were. I started to panic that my suit might a) make me visible to the protestors' anger and b) get all eggy from all the eggs.

Everyone started to take the piss out of me for being in a suit. I then realised that time was getting on and that I had been at the protest a full 30 minutes over my allocated lunch time. Chief told me to have my last few tugs on a spliff before I left the carnage of the protest to skedaddle back at the office.

My colleagues were eager to find out how I managed to get back in the building alive. I lied and told them that it had been quite a peaceful protest and there wasn't much going on. Being very stoned, and pissed, I then told them that I didn't have time to speak to anyone, as I had some urgent work that needed to be finished before the end of the day. I don't think they believed me, but office etiquette meant that nobody questioned me and they left me alone for the rest of the afternoon. I then spent the next four hours staring at my screen in a daze, avoiding eye contact with anyone and everyone in the office, and pretending to be doing something productive that would help keep those wheels of capitalism turning.

31.
PIRANHA

Being stuck in the middle of the sweaty, humid Amazon jungle, meant it didn't take long for me and Keels to stink like orangutans in a sauna. Zacambu wasn't exactly the type of place you could slip into a nice warm bath or have a nice refreshing shower. Our stench had obviously made an impression, as our guide, Raymond approached us both and told us to jump in the river.

"Er, no, you're alright, Raymond. Don't piranhas live in this river?"

"Is OK," he said. "Lots of piranha. Black and red-bellied piranha bad, but not here. Only good piranha. Attack only if bleed."

Keels and I checked our bodies for any cuts, desperately hoping to find one so that we could excuse ourselves from bathing in the water.

"You come," said Raymond, motioning us into the river.

We looked at the river. The village kids I had previously been throwing around, were now all happily swimming, and playing in the water. I turned to Keels.

"Mon. We've got to do it."

"Fuck that, Wev."

"Look, mon. All of the kids are in there. We'll look like a right couple of numpties if we don't go in."

"I don't care. I ain't fucking jumping in that river."

"We do fucking stink though."

"Yeah, we do."

I shouted over to Raymond to tell him that we would be in shortly, then went into my rucksack and pulled out my trusty papaya extract hair-thickening formula shampoo and took it down to the rickety jetty. Keels and I stood nervously at the river's edge, when suddenly, the fat cunt gave me a big shove and I fell head first into the river. I came back up panicked and gasping for air, only to find the village kids, Keels and Raymond all pointing at me, laughing. The kids then proceeded to swim over to me, climb on me and use me as a diving board. As I stood there motionless, I felt a few nibbles on my leg.

"What the fuck?"

The nibbles turned into bites.

"Raymond? I thought you said the piranhas won't attack us. They're fucking biting me."

Raymond laughed. "Yes. They bite, but not attack."

"What's the fucking difference?"

Raymond laughed again. Keels backed away from the river's edge.

As I was splashing about, making a scene, desperate to pull myself up on to of the jetty, flying fish started to fly out the water. There were tens of them launching out of the water around me, trying to get away.

"Ha-ha. Fish fly to escape piranha," Raymond said, laughing.

I eventually calmed down, and tried to focus on how the piranha bites felt on my legs and torso. Not quite nibbles, not quite bites, I ended up calling them "nips" as you could certainly feel the famous teeth, if only fleetingly: the word "piranha" means literally "tooth fish" in the Tupí language.

32.
PISSED-OFF PALACE

One night in the early nineties (don't ask me when exactly), I had been to see a Nick Cave gig in London with Kotch and missed the last train back to Dartford. This happened to me a few times and was always a complete pain in the arse. The only way home would be via a night bus, but these only ran every hour, with the journey lasting a full hour and a half. They were never particularly fun, as they would be packed full of really loud, pissed and lairy people (us included) and there would always be a chance that fights would break out on them. We learned that the best thing to do would be to forget about getting on a bus any time before 2am, as that was when the majority of drunk knobends would be on their way home. Any bus after that time would generally consist of people out their heads on drugs or people so pissed that they would just fall asleep and cause no mischief.

We left the Nick Cave gig at the Astoria in Tottenham Court Road around midnight, out of our heads on booze and acid, and stumbled down to the bus stop at Trafalgar Square. The place was rammed full of greasy, hot-dog-munching reprobates. I got the fear and didn't want to hang around the bus stop whilst there were so many fighty drunkards there, so suggested to Kotch that we go for a walk in St James' Park. We had a few spliffs on us, so we could keep ourselves entertained. We left Trafalgar Square and the hordes of nonsense behind us and walked through Admiralty Arch, where we could see Buckingham Palace glowing in the distance at the other end of The Mall, with St James' Park on our left.

We sat next to the lake, skinned up a spliff and spent the next

20 minutes talking shit. I then came up with the bright idea of paying Buckingham Palace a little visit. Kotch agreed, so we skirted the banks of the lake until it was in view. I am far from a royalist, but the palace looked amazing, with the dark lake and silhouette of trees before us and the brightly lit palace looming over the lake and trees. It's beauty almost brought tears to my acid-infused eyes. I then noticed that the flag was raised.

"Kotch. The flag's raised. You know what that means?"

"No."

"Lizzie is in."

"Wicked, mon. Let's throw stones at her window and try to wake her up."

We reached the front gates and stood there for a couple of minutes. Desperation for a piss suddenly descended upon me. I promptly slapped my cock out and started pissing through the gates and into the courtyard in front of the palace. Very proud of myself, I decided to push my respect for the monarch up a notch, by shouting, "God Save the Queen, the fascist regime!" at the top of my lungs. Kotch started cracking up with laughter. This egged me on to shout it out a couple of times more. I finished my wet act of vandalism and slipped my knob back in my pants.

I then noticed a shadowy presence behind me. I turned and saw a policeman on the other side of the gate walk closer towards me, until he stepped directly into my large piss puddle.

That would have pissed him off, for sure.

"What are you two doing here?" he bellowed.

"'Ello, 'ello, 'ello," we bellowed back, thinking that we were being very original with our quips.

The rozzer was unamused. "What are you two doing here?"

"Just paying Dizzy Miss Lizzie the respect she deserves," I said.

"Do you think you're funny?" the policeman replied.

Being out of my head on acid and not exactly thinking before speaking, I came back at the police officer with something I regretted immediately.

"Not at all, guvnor. You're the funny one protecting that cunt."

This brought an instant response of the policeman chattering into his walkie-talkie thang. Unbeknownst to Kotch and I, two burly officers, about 30 metres behind me, had been slowly waiting for the signal.

"Let's get the fuck out of here!" I yelled.

We both ran for our lives back into St James' Park, quickly followed by the two police officers. It was quite terrifying. We would have gone to the clink for sure, or even the Tower. We ran as fast as we could, powered by booze and acid, all the while laughing our stupid little heads off. I would have thought that being beyond inhibited meant our running skills would have suffered, but we easily outran the police. Though, they probably thought we weren't worth the effort of a chase.

The good thing about St James' Park is that, unlike most parks in Central London, there are lots of bushes around the lake, so quite a few potential hiding places. We decided to keep on running until we reached the opposite end of the park to the palace, by Horse Guard's Parade. We darted into some bushes around there and sat there giggling for at least 30 minutes, until we deemed it safe to walk back to Trafalgar Square. As we walked back to the bus stop, I noticed that we were standing round the back of Downing Street and, as luck would have it, I needed another piss.

33.
CRACK TRAIN

It was just an average Saturday morning at the squat in Bethnal Green, as Danger, Bon and I happily listened to Spiritualized in a drug-soaked daze. We started the day with the heroin that was left from the previous night's adventures. We each chased our very own little brown dragon across some tin foil, until there was none left, and our brains were a heavily sedated mush. Once the brown was finished and the onset of puking came, we started on the ketamine. Of course, we couldn't have a ket session without some crack, so we pulled out some household ammonia and a couple of grams of coke and rustled up a few rocks, to accompany us through the k-hole. We were fucking nutted.

"Shall we go to Canterbury?" I announced, out of nowhere.

The boys looked at me strangely. More strangely than normal.

"Canterbury is really nice. It's got a lot of history and some wall that goes around it. I reckon we should pay it a little visit."

Bon was sold on the idea. He loved walls. "Let's do it."

Danger wasn't convinced. "Don't you want to just chill here and get out of our heads?"

"Come on, you lazy cunt," I said standing up. "We can take the drugs with us."

The three of us were out the house by 11am, with an ounce of skunk weed, a couple of grams of ketamine, a few rocks of crack, a couple of grams of coke and a few bottles of vodka. As we started walking down the Old Ford Road, Danger asked me how we will get to Canterbury.

"A train, I suppose."

I was mullered, but I've always been good with directions, no matter how out of my head I am. I managed to direct us from Bethnal Green to London Bridge train station without many mishaps, apart from the obligatory walking into walls and strangers. We arrived at London Bridge Station and checked out a train map. All the lines on the map started moving, wiggling, pulsating. It was remarkably interesting, but not conducive to our goal of finding out how to get to Canterbury, so we looked at the timetable that was conveniently positioned next to the map. This helped us even less. The black letters and numbers jumped off the background, and started dancing; none of it made any sense. How the fuck were we supposed to get to Canterbury, if the maps and timetables weren't any good? Fucking British Rail cunts. The amount of money I'd invested in them through the taxes I'd paid, and they couldn't even sort us out with decent maps or timetables with words and numbers that didn't wriggle about. Bon suggested to ask the person at the ticket office when we bought our tickets.

The tickets were purchased, and directions were given. We had to travel to Chatham first, then change for another train to Canterbury and the whole journey would take nearly two hours. I started regretting coming up with the suggestion of a visit to Canterbury. It seemed like a lot of work. Seeing as the tickets were already purchased, we decided to commit to the journey and made our way up to the platform, walking to the very end. We had 10 minutes to wait for the train, so decided to roll up a one skin each of tobacco, skunk, a few sprinkles of ketamine, and a few crumbs of crack. On consumption of this little metallic-tasting beauty, the regret disappeared and the oddness of being so out of my head, but in a very mundane situation of being at a train station, surrounded by "normal" people, filled my mind with joy.

We spent the journey to Chatham, predominantly in the shit-smelling toilet, taking turns to smoke more than a few crack-ketamine roll-ups. Stupidly, we thought that the fact we weren't smoking the potent-smelling skunk weed, would mean that nobody would know we were smoking in the bogs. We were so out of our nuts, we thought we were being discreet with our drug taking. In reality, the carriage stank. It was horrific. Everybody was probably too terrified to say anything to us though, and we continued until we reached Chatham an hour later.

If you've never smoked crack on a very busy train before – and hopefully you haven't – it's everything you expect it to be. It's the happiest I've ever been on a train.

We all stumbled off the train and on to the connecting train to Canterbury. This time, we couldn't find a toilet to smoke in, so had to spend the next 40 minutes drug free. We were obviously being quite loud and stupid, because Danger produced a very loud, wet fart from his arsehole. I cracked up laughing.

The smell was – well, you can imagine.

"Danger, that's rank."

We all then looked at a woman with a child. She looked extremely pale. All three of us just couldn't help but start laughing. The lady's face went a deep crimson. She then whispered something to her child and they both stood up and walked out of our lives, to a different part of the carriage. This obviously made us laugh even more.

On arrival into Canterbury, we realised we weren't in any fit state to walk too far from the train station, so parked ourselves in a park approximately two minutes' walk from the station (but next to the wall). The next four hours were spent in much the same vein as the journey – smoking crack, and farting.

When day turned to dusk, we decided it was time to return to London. We all stumbled back on to the return train to Chatham and sunk deeply into our seats, very content with the day's excursion, despite seeing none of beautiful Canterbury. We did, however, see fart lady and her small child again.

Mental monkeys...

...on Monkey Mountain

34.
MONKEY MASSACRE

My newfound half-brother, Ian, and his girl-friend, Jules, came to visit me whilst I was living in Hong Kong. Whenever I had visitors, I always made sure a trip to the heavily forested hills of Monkey Mountain were a part of the itinerary. Seeing as it was my brother's first trip outside of Europe, I thought we should make this an extra special occasion. So, I packed a bag full of fruit to feed to the monkeys.

We hailed a cab in Mongkok, which dropped us off at the Monkey Mountain bus stop. On the left-hand side of the road, is a track that leads you down to a reservoir. That's where all the monkeys congregate. On the right-hand side is a dirt pathway that leads up to the top of a hill for an amazing vista of the Hong Kong metropolis. Most days, the view is obscured by the general smog and pollution that comes from the city, but if you get there on a clear day, it is a sight you won't see anywhere else on Earth. We weren't going there for the view, though. We were there so that Ian could feed the monkeys. So we started heading down the track that led to the reservoir.

Most of the fruit we had bought was safely tucked away in a backpack. However, we had bought too much fruit for it all to fit in the bag, so Ian was also carrying a plastic bag with a few apples and bananas. I asked Ian if he could hand me the bag of fruit, so I would be ready to feed the monkeys from my hand, and reduce the chances of them going after my backpack. It happens.

Of course, holding the fruit soon became a very bad idea. After walking 10 metres from the main road, I had now been spotted, harassed and stalked by a dozen or so of the more alert monkeys, who had clocked what I was carrying in the plastic bag. Fearing for my safety, I pulled an apple out. Before I had a chance to throw it at the oncoming flurry of monkeys, one of the larger fuckers jumped in front of me and ripped a big hole out of the plastic bag, before grabbing the apple out of my other hand. I pushed him off me and saw all of the fruit in my bag fall out of the hole and roll towards him as he sat munching away at the apple a few feet away.

Now that these monkeys thought we were fruit-less, they left us alone. We carried on walking down towards the reservoir and managed to get pretty close to a few monkey families. It was quite heart-warming, standing there watching them delouse each other, play together, and scratch each other's arses. The little baby monklets – as I call them – are really cute and have massive ears and small heads. Unfortunately, their ear-to-head ratio decreases with age, so the cuteness factor soon subsides.

We noticed a poster stuck against a rock face, stating that you should not bring food to Monkey Mountain. Feeding the animals has resulted in a lot more monkey attacks on humans and subsequently more complaints about the rude and aggressive behaviour of the monkeys.

"Let's feed the monkeys the rest of the fruit," I whispered to Ian and Jules, with a devilish grin. As you should know by now, if I see a sign that tells me not to do something, chances are it's too late – I've already done it. Monkey see, monkey do, if you will.

I took off the backpack and pulled out two large, full bags of apples, oranges, and bananas. This fruitopia led a couple of inquisitive and knowledgeable monkeys to me, where I threw out a couple of apples. Within seconds, there were – and this is nowhere near an exaggeration – more than 200 monkeys approaching us from every direction. Within thirty seconds, I was surrounded. Ian and Jules backed away from me. As the monkeys advanced on me, I saw a conveniently placed broken tree branch on the floor. I picked it up and started beating off the monkeys – not like that

– as I frantically tried to throw every last bit of fruit from my bag as far away from me as possible, before they finally overpowered me with sheer numbers. Some of the larger monkeys managed to get past my stick and shove defence. Two of them were on my body, grabbing at each other and at the fruit that I was holding, looking in the bag, snuffling for more. I managed to beat them both off – not like that – but that just made them more persistent.

I managed to rid myself of all the fruit I had and beat a further four to five monkeys off – not like that – just to regain my footing. I had monkeys under my feet. After a wrestle with one of the bigger ones, the monkeys finally realised I had no more fruit left and stopped hassling me. I took a step back and looked at the carnage around me. The floor underneath the "Do Not Feed The Monkeys" sign was littered with lots of monkeys, fruit, and vegetables.

The chaos wasn't over, though.

Now, it was the time for the monkey in-fighting.

The larger monkeys started pushing the smaller monkeys away from the fruit on the floor. Some of the smaller ones just took a couple of small handfuls of fruit and scurried away into the trees. The stupid monkeys tried to stand their ground and got a face full of claws and sharp teeth.

It was a massacre. A monkey massacre. All hell had broken loose. The noise alone – of scores of screaming, angry monkeys – was the sound of nightmares.

Imagine it. Hundreds of monkeys fighting just a few feet away from us.

A few limped away with fresh cuts and bruises until all that was left on the track was about five, big old fuckers, each surrounded by a few pools of blood and a small pile of fruit each that they had stolen from the other monkeys.

Feeling extremely guilty about the scene I had started, I told Ian and Jules that it was time to leave. Once the food runs out, they could turn on us. At least, that was my logic.

We edged our way past the alpha monkeys, as they munched

through the spoils of war. We looked up in the trees, at the less fortunate ones and noticed a few with scores of scars and missing eyes and limbs. "Frigging hell, Monkey Mountain is a war zone!" Jules yelled.

We took the path back to the road amidst the sickening screams of monkey's beating each other off violently. Not like that.

Beach Boys

35.
TWO SQUADDIES

I've never been a violent man, or a bully. I abhor the toxic, testosterone-fuelled, alpha-male masculinity that you find on your average football terrace or suburban town. Unfortunately, it hasn't meant that I have been able to avoid violence. The instance I am about to describe is not my proudest moment. Which, considering the contents of this book, is really saying something.

It was the early nineties and Chief and I had been on a vinyl record spending spree in London's Soho and were on the train back to Dartford. We were sitting on the train, excited about playing our new tunes on my turntables at home, when we overheard a raucous conversation a bit further down the carriage. We instantly became a bit subdued and fearful that a fight was going to kick off on the train. There was extremely loud swearing and abuse being shouted between a couple of fellow passengers.

As the train trundled along, we heard a kerfuffle between two men, with lots of drunken yelling.

"Shit. It's properly kicking off over there," I said.

"Yeah. Just keep your loud mouth shut, Wev. We don't want them starting on us," Chief responded. He knows I have a proclivity for trouble to find me.

"I ain't a fucking idiot," I retaliated.

"Unfortunately, you are. Just don't do anything to piss them off, like say hello. Just keep quiet and look out the window."

I took Chief's wise words on board and kept my mouth shut for the rest of the journey. The train finally pulled into Dartford station and we alighted from the train. The two hoodlums in the carriage ahead of us also left the train at the same time as us. As we walked down the platform, we heard a shout from one of them. I turned around and saw they were two squaddies.

Forgetting my vow of silence, I greeted them, as I do any stranger. "Alright there, mons?"

"Mons? Who you fucking calling 'mons'?" said Squaddie #1, laughing.

Chief looked at me in disbelief and shouted to them, "Yeah. Don't worry about him lads, he's a cock."

"Yeah. A major mon-cock if you ask me," said Squaddie #2.

We both turned around and increased our walking speed. We then started hearing chants coming from behind us.

"Mon-cock. Mon-cock. Mons, mons, mons," sang Squaddie #1 and Squaddie #2 together.

Chief whispered to me, "Yeah, nice one, Wev. Look what you've started."

We heard a bit of movement behind us. I turned around and saw the two squaddies pushing and shoving each other. They saw me looking at them, then shouted. "What you looking at, mons?"

The fear took hold. This was about to get violent. My dumbshit sense was tingling.

"You don't think they're going to beat us up, do ya?"

Chief just kept his head down.

Our walking pace quickened to a trot. The squaddies noticed this and shouted. "Don't fucking run away from us, mon-fuckers. We'll run after you." They then started laughing.

Chief then suddenly started running.

I almost ran after him but feared this would prompt a mad sprint between us and the squaddies that would end with our faces becoming intimate with their fists.

To confuse them, I slowed my pace down. If anything, I started to skip.

As I left the train station a minute or so later, I saw Chief running back towards the train station from our local boozer, the Chug Chug Tavern. He wasn't on his own, though. He was closely followed by a big, fat, eight-foot-tall biker geezer we knew from the pub called Mark. Being rotund, Mark was finding the running quite difficult, and was a sweating and wheezing mass of blubber. Chief pointed at the two squaddies, who were now about ten metres behind us, and shouted to Mark, "That's them!"

Mark bouldered over to them. "Problem?" he said, calmly.

Before the squaddies had a chance to respond, Mark had thrown a punch straight in the face of Squaddie #2 with his right hand and a head butt in the face of Squaddie #1. The squaddies both crumpled to the floor with their hands to their heads.

Mark ignored their screams and booted them both in the stomach a couple of times. The squaddies shouted again; blood was now puddling on the ground.

I was looking at them writhing around in pain on the floor and felt terrible. How did a simple "Alright there, mons?" come to this? I shouted to Mark, "Please stop. They didn't actually start on us or anything. They were just pissed wankers!"

"They shouted shit, but that's all," I said.

Mark looked at the squaddies on the floor. "Oh," is all he said, before walking away back to the pub. Mark didn't do apologies.

The squaddies looked up at Mark, with blood streaming from their faces, and tried to stand.

Chief and I left the squaddies on the ground and walked to the boozer with Mark. On entry to the pub, all Mark said of the matter was, "Fuckin' squaddies," before returning to his pint.

Green leaves...

...White powder

36.
GREEN COKE

Keels and I were in the Colombian border town of Leticia. We decided to hire a motorbike and see where the one road out of town would lead us. It was a hot and humid day. At the 11-kilometre mark, we saw a number of locals hanging around a hut, so decided to see what was happening. The tiny hut was a bar. We decided to check it out. We greedily consumed three local beers, four cakes and three bags of South American crisps each within 45 minutes. As we munched and slurped our way through our food and drink, a local desperado wandered in and ordered himself a beer. He promptly downed the beer in one and then, rather unexpectedly, ran out of the bar without paying. The proprietor of the joint chased after him, caught up with him easily, threw him down to the ground and then beat him around the head a few times. The drunkard was left crumpled on the floor in the road. The bar owner returned, cursing. We immediately paid our bill.

The half-dozen other people in the bar burst out laughing at the sight of the desperado lying bloodied on the dusty ground. Most of the clientele in this place looked to be of Indian descent. Keels and I spotted that one of our fellow drinkers was sniffing quite a lot. He must be a coca fiend. This poor chap also had a gammy eye, with gunk and tears streaming out of it. I always carried around eye drops, as they could clear the bloodshot eyes that I always got from substance abuse. I showed this to the man, and Keels explained what it was as he could speak the language. He then promptly applied it to his dodgy eye.

Next thing you know, we've got a new friend.

He then produced a bag of green powder out of his pocket.

"Coca," he said.

"Really?"

"Coca."

"But it's green," I responded, wary.

"Natural coca. Pure. You come my house."

His house wasn't far from the bar, so we walked the motorbike round there and met his wife and 12 kids. We noticed that one of his children had the same gammy-eye problem, and I offered my eye drops to the boy. The man was happy. So, happy, he showed us his garden of delights.

The first plant he introduced us to was an antiseptic plant. He pulled off some leaves, handed them to us, then motioned for us to rub them up and down our severely mosquito-bitten arms. We rubbed the leaves up and down our forearms. On application, our arms stung terribly, then started bubbling.

"Is OK. Medicine," he reassured.

Keels and I looked in horror as our arms bubbled. However, a minute or so later, once the stinging and the bubbling subsided, the mozzy bites were reduced to nothing. Amazing. Unfortunately, I never asked the man what the name of the plant was so when I tell people of the bubbling skin and then the disappearing mozzy bites, I am generally met with an element of disbelief.

The stranger then showed us another plant that he was growing. He told Keels that when the bark is mixed with water and consumed, "it will allow you to see into the future". Naturally, this sparked my interest. "Apparently, it leaves you out of your mind for five days," said Keels. As we were leaving for Iquitos the following day, I unfortunately did not get a chance to try that one out. Again, I didn't ask the name of it.

He then introduced us to his coca plants. He had about 10 in total. He picked a few handfuls of green leaves from the plants, then heated them in a big silver pan over a fire until they were dried. He then crumbled them in a mortar and pestle and ground the remains. He picked another bunch of leaves from a tree that looked like a very large sycamore tree and heated them over the fire. He then mixed the ashes of those with the powdered coca leaves.

He went into his wooden hut and came back with a dirty old sock. He poured the dry, powdered leaves into the sock and used it to filter all the powder back into the silver pan. He then found a spoon, spooned up a load of the powder and stuck it in his mouth. He left it in his mouth for about 20 seconds, then opened his mouth to show us the powder had turned to liquid with his saliva. Once he had this pool of green swill in his mouth, he swallowed.

He then handed the spoon to me and within a few seconds I had a very numb mouth. This was definitely recognisable to the numbing effects of cocaine when you rub it on your gums. The high you get from cocaine wasn't there, though, and the buzz to this was quite chilled even though the numbness was of similar strength. I then followed his demonstration of the whole process, which took about 10 minutes, and made my own batch of coca. We stayed at his house for a couple of hours, mixing and making a few batches, chatting and ingesting a few more spoonfuls of green coca powder. We now had quite a decent buzz on. I was thrilled that I had had the opportunity to make pure, natural "cocaine" – all thanks to the eye drops.

It had grown quite late in the afternoon and we decided it was time to leave before it became too dark. He hurried over to the metal pan and spooned up a sizeable portion of the green powder into a small container and handed it to us. We gave each other hugs, exchanged addresses, then we threw his mass of children the international sign of Britishness: the double thumbs up.

We rode back down the road to Leticia, and yet somehow completely missed the town. I blame the green cocaine. We ended up crossing the border into Brazil and went riding off into the Brazilian jungle. With the container of coca powder in my pocket, this officially made us narcotics traffickers, though there was no one around to give a fuck.

lost in the desert

37.
WANKER DRIVER

It was the late nineties when I was at the peak of my drug taking hedonism. One night during that time, while living at the squat in Bethnal Green, we ran out of ganja. Our dealer in Dartford told us there was a drought and he couldn't sort us out for another week. This obviously caused big turbulence within the household. Conversation ground to a halt, the laughter stopped, and panicked expressions spread across everyone's straight faces.

We had a few bags full of seeds and dust we had collected from past buds that we started to smoke, but got us nowhere near where we needed to be. Bon spent the night sifting through these bags; Danger went on a treasure hunt around every nook and cranny in the house, as he was known for hiding drug paraphernalia and forgetting where he had hidden it. I opened the vacuum cleaner bag and sifted through the rubbish and dust in the vain hope that something had been sucked up over the last few weeks. All this effort yielded zero results.

I then remembered my friend Gussy, who lived in Camberwell, and had come up trumps on previous occasions when we'd run dry. I called her up and she told me she could get half an ounce of skunk for me the following day. With that sorted, we all decided that it was too depressing trying to talk to each other sober, so bid each other goodnight and went to bed.

At this time in our lives, we were all of the impression that we couldn't sleep without the help of a healthy amount of THC (the active ingredient in weed) coursing through our veins. It took every one of us hours to get to sleep that night, as we laid in our respective pits, thinking about not being able to sleep because we had not smoked any weed. It was tantamount to torture.

I woke at 7.30am and made my way to the office for a day at work. All I could think about was leaving the office after work and smoking spliffs. My productivity levels were non-existent, as I couldn't get the thought of scoring some weed and having a good old time out of my mind. It finally reached 5.30pm and I promptly left the office and made my way to Gussy's house in Camberwell Green. When I arrived at her house, her fella, Scram, let me in. The three of us spent a good couple of hours smoking and talking nonsense. I was sedated and I was happy. I then received a panicked phone call on my brand-new Nokia 95.

"Wev! Where the fuck are you?"

It was Danger.

"Uh? You know where I am. I'm at Gussy's house."

"Did you get the skunk?"

"Yeah. It's well nice."

"Just hurry the fuck home, will ya? We're all desperate here and you're sitting there stoned out your mind. You're out of order!"

"Alright, mon. Calm down. I'll leave in a minute. I'll be back in about an hour."

"Just hurry up."

I put the phone down, then rolled and smoked a farewell spliff with Gussy and Scram. I thanked them both profusely for helping a friend in need.

I was about halfway down Camberwell New Road when a car pulled up beside me. I didn't notice it at first, but it moved at my walking pace and flashed its lights a couple of times, until I finally noticed. (I was lost in the middle of the 10-minute-long and very deep blues tune called "Amandrai" by Ali Farka Toure on my Sony Walkman, I seem to recall.) I stopped the music but wasn't happy about it.

"Can I help you, mate?"

"Yes. I need to go to New Cross. Do you know how to get there?"

"Yeah, just keep going straight," I said. "If you stay on this road, you will get there in about 15 minutes."

"Thanks."

With that, I turned away and got my Sony Walkman out of my pocket, so that I could lose myself in music again.

"Er, mate. Seeing as you were so helpful," the voice came back. "Do you want me to drop you off anywhere?"

Remembering the stressful sounds of Dr Danger on the phone, I thought the music could wait and this geezer could drop me off at the bus stop.

"Yeah. Could you just drop me off at those traffic lights further up the road?"

"Of course. Jump in."

I jumped into the passenger seat at the front of the car.

"So, where are you off to?"

"I'm going to Bethnal Green."

"Bethnal Green? Where's that?"

"East London."

"That's a long way. Do you want me to drive you there?"

"What?" I scoffed.

"I'm early for my appointment, so I could drop you off in Bethnal Green first and still be on time for my meeting in New Cross."

"But Bethnal is on the other side of the river? It's miles away from New Cross."

"Don't worry about it. As I said, I'm early."

"Alright, then. Fair play."

The kindness of strangers does exist!

I shook my new friend's hand.

He drove right through Camberwell, Peckham, New Cross and Deptford, then crossed the river via the Rotherhithe Tunnel. We were about ten minutes from the squat, when the man turned to me and said the second-worst sentence I have ever heard.

"Would you like to wank yourself off?"

I stared at him in horror.

"What?"

"Would you like to wank yourself off?"

193

"No," was all I dared muster.

"Oh. OK."

There was an uncomfortable silence for a minute or so. And then he said the worst sentence I have ever heard.

"Would you mind driving so that I could wank myself off?"

"What?"

"I'm wondering whether you could drive so that I can wank myself off."

"Mate. No, sorry, I can't drive."

"Oh, I'm really sorry."

"Can you just take me home?"

"Oh, yes. Of course. I'm really sorry."

There was obviously a great deal of complete silence for the rest of the journey. He finally pulled up outside the squat.

I jumped out the car and mumbled "thanks" sheepishly.

I left him staring at me from the car as I stumbled through the front door. As soon as I entered, the lads pounced on me.

"You got the herb? You got the herb?"

"Calm down, you twats. I've got one hell of a story to tell you all."

I took out the bag of weed from my pocket and placed it in the middle of the kitchen table. Everyone sat down and started busily building their own spliffs. I then regaled them with my tale of woe.

A couple of minutes passed in a hazy and contented silence, then Bon walked over to the window. "Erm, he's still there," Bon said. We all rushed over to the window to see. And, yep, the guy was still sitting in the car outside the squat.

And, then, it dawned on us all at the same time why he was still there. "Trouble really does follow you home, doesn't it?" laughed Bon.

"Shut the curtains, will ya?" I cried out as I rolled my much-needed spliff.

38.
THE BRIBE

I t was the mid-noughties. I took Danger to Venezuela for a month-long crack session to help him kick his own heroin habit. Fuzzy logic, maybe. But logic, nonetheless.

One day, we were sitting on a beach in Porlamar, the main town in Margarita Island. Margarita Island is a popular tourist resort for middle-aged Speedo-wearing Europeans, although they tend to frequent the beaches on the east coast of the island in all-inclusive hotels. This particular beach was in the middle of town and frequented by local crack heads and rabid dogs called "Chicken".

We had previously scored some weed from one of the crack dealers and were happily turning our pasty-white bodies into a scorched scarlet red as we smoked and vegetated on our T-shirts while sunbathing on the beach. Danger had just rolled the mother of all bifters and sparked it up, when I noticed a couple of blokes walking towards us.

"Danger? Do you reckon those geezers are coming over to us?"

"Eh?" Danger lazily looked over to the men, who had by now started trotting in our direction.

"Rozzers," Danger said calmly.

We looked around us. Cops. Shit. Not only did Danger have a spliff the size of an elephant's cock in his mouth, but we also had about half an ounce of weed sunbathing between us.

I sat up straight and started digging a hole. It was absolutely pointless. By the time it took us to sit up, the rozzers were already standing over us, watching us busily try to bury our very illegal drugs. We stopped when we heard a booming voice start gibbering

195

to us in Spanish. I looked up at the two police officers and offered a very meek, "Que? Inglesi?"

They laughed, then one of them barked. "What you do?"

"Er, we're just sunbathing," I offered.

"What this?" he said, picking up the bag of weed.

"Marijuana."

"This illegal."

"What? Is it? I thought it was OK to smoke weed here."

"No. You in big trouble."

"Shit. What are you going to do?"

"You. Big trouble," He replied, looking more serious than I would have liked.

The police officers then laughed. That was not the response I expected. I started having visions of me and Danger spending the rest of our days in a cockroach-infested Venezuelan prison, with only the butt-fucking by the local mafioso to look forward to.

The policeman laughed again. "You in trouble. What you do now?"

"Go to prison?" I offered in response.

The policeman sighed, then asked again. "What you do now?"

Danger finally piped up and said something dangerous.

"20 US dollars?"

The police officers laughed.

"$30," Danger said, cool as fuck. (It was only much later that I realised that he knew what was going on here.)

The police officers laughed.

"$50…" said Danger.

The police officers didn't laugh.

"$100," I blurted nervously.

The police officers laughed loudly and shoved out their hands.

I rummaged around in my pocket, pulled out two crisp $50 notes and handed it over to one of the police officers. He handed me back the bag of weed. Happy with their bribe, the two police officers strolled off, cackling.

Danger turned to me, angry. "You're such an idiot, Wev… they would have taken $50."

39.
TICK THE DICK

I was out on the razz down the King's Road, Chelsea, at some point in the nineties with Keels (prior to his move to Colombia). We decided that the aim for the day was to visit every bar that we stumbled upon and order the most expensive (and therefore most alcoholic) cocktail on offer. We also agreed that we should stop off at every back alley or hidden spot we passed and smoke some premium greenery. After our sixth cocktail and our third spliff, our heads were obviously quite mashed.

I spotted some sort of market in a converted warehouse. I told Keels I wanted to check it out, as I needed a new pair of jeans all of a sudden. We stumbled in and were confronted with several trendy, looking clothes stalls, so I started perusing some racks in the first shop we came upon. Whilst I was searching through the clothes and gibbering nonsense to Keels in my usual high decibels, I noticed that we were being stalked by the shop assistant.

"What the fuck do you reckon that geezer wants?" I said.

"What geezer?"

"The weird punk who keeps on following us. Do you reckon he thinks we're going to steal something?"

Keels turned and looked at the punk. The bloke wasn't an actual punk but was one of those trendy types that would spend hours every morning doing their hair and clothes to have a punky vibe about them. He sported multi-coloured blue, black, and red hair, spiked and gelled to the heavens in a plethora of different angles, had lots of piercings in his ears, nose, and eyebrows and wore tattered designer clothes, that obviously cost him a fortune.

I looked at him. He looked at me. He gave me a smile. I grinned back then turned to the clothes I was looking through. My grin must have given the shop assistant the confidence to approach me and talk, as the next thing I knew, he was invading my personal space, and asking me whether I needed any help in an OTT, camp middle-class accent. The juxtaposition of punk and public school threw me off my people-spotting skills. This guy was too much of everything. I told him that I was looking for some jeans. He grabbed my hand and told me that he had just the pair that would look perfect on me.

I sensed that this super-styled gentleman had taken a fancy to little ol' me. The way he smiled and batted his eye lids made me think he was all mine if I wanted.

He led me, by the hand, to another rack of jeans, where he produced a pair of black antique-wash Levi's. They were really nice, to be fair. I then looked at the price tag. 50 quid. Fuck that.

Then a thought came into my mind.

A dumb-shit idea.

One of my worst.

If I flirted with the bloke a little, I thought, he might offer me a staff discount or even a generous savings. I tried on the jeans in the fitting rooms, then came back out to the shop and asked him how they looked. Thankfully, Keels had grown bored and was waiting outside the shop.

"They look great," the assistant said.

"Are you sure?" I flirted. "They don't make my bum look big, do they?"

I turned my back to him and slowly stroked my arse.

"No. No. Not at all," he smiled. "Your bum looks… fantastic."

"Oh. Thanks. You are kind," I said with a wink. "I really like these jeans, but they are a little expensive."

I then told him that I wasn't sure I could afford the jeans and would think about the purchase, whilst I changed back into my old jeans. I turned and walked back to the changing rooms, ensuring that I swayed my hips, and gave him a show. I could feel, his eyes burning a hole in my buttocks. Once I was changed, I made my way back to him and handed him back the jeans. I ensured I accidentally stroked my fingers along his hand. "If only…" I said softly.

"I'll give you a discount," he said. "How much can you pay?"

"30 quid?"

"That's quite a big discount," he said, his face contorted. "Sorry…"

"Oh, it's OK. Maybe one day…"

I turned to leave, but he grabbed my hand. "OK. OK. £30. *For you.*"

I turned back to him. "Oh, thank you so much. Aren't you amazing?"

My flirting was turned all the way up to 11.

"OK. Come to the counter and pay," he said, before adding, "I have something else you might like to see."

I followed him to the counter, handed over money in exchange for my lovely new jeans in a plastic bag. I was feeling very proud of myself. Until, in one swift movement, he handed me a photograph, he pulled from his back pocket.

"What do you think of this?"

I looked down at the photo. It was a picture of a large erect cock. With a ring pierced through the head.

I gulped and spluttered, unsure of where to divert my eyes.

I looked at the photo again and then wished I hadn't. He then handed me a notepad and pen, with four columns.

Love

Like

Don't Like

Don't Mind

I could see a few ticks had been ticked in each of the columns.

I handed him back the notepad, pen, and photograph. I ticked "Don't Like" and simply walked out of the shop. I couldn't even turn back to say goodbye.

"Let's grab a cocktail," said Keels as I walked out the door.

"I've had enough," I snapped, as Keels looked at me strangely.

No caption necessary

40.
ACID QUEUE

Back in the days when illegal raves were legal, I went to one in King's Cross, London, with my sister, Woo, and her mate, Letch. My sister and her friends were the original ravers, spending the late eighties and early nineties out of their heads, travelling around the UK, finding shindigs where you could freely take the new drug on the scene: ecstasy. House music was also the new kid on the block and was the main vibe that went on down at these raves. I was a couple of years too young to be a raver (plus I've never been into house music), but on the rare occasion my sister invited me to join her and her friends to a rave, I would always jump at the chance.

Letch picked us both up from my parents house at 10pm and drove us to London. Woo wanted us all to be well and truly "on one" when we arrived. She wanted to show me the true rave experience and wanted to get in the thick of it as soon as possible, rather than waiting to come up on our choice of drugs for the evening. With this in mind, we chain smoked weed for the duration of the car journey and downed a microdot of acid each when we were 20 minutes from the venue.

We arrived in King's Cross, Letch parked the car, and we made our way to an abandoned warehouse behind the train station. As we were walking along the road, I started feeling the effects of the acid. I was coming up like a trooper. I looked at Woo and Letch. Their eyes were popping out of their heads. These must have been strong old acid tabs, as I normally wouldn't have felt these effects for at least another 20 minutes. When we arrived at the entrance to the rave, we were confronted with a sea of people. I couldn't understand what was going on. There were just shitloads of people, who looked equally as fucked as us.

As soon as we joined the throngs of people, I felt a surge through my brain and a stickiness in my throat. Fuck. The acid was pushing up to the next level of other-worldliness. People were getting impatient with the queue, and started pushing and shoving. The waves of LSD in my brain were moving in rhythm with the sweating mass of people, trying to get into the rave. Woo and Letch were shoved ten metres in front of me. I could see them, but I couldn't get anywhere near them, as there were too many sweaty blokes wearing bucket hats and smiley face T-shirts between us. I was going to have to deal with this on my own.

I looked around. There were literally hundreds of people surrounding me. An ocean of neon clothing and perspiration. Woo shouted out to me and I gave her the thumbs up, although I really wasn't enjoying myself. I wanted to get the fuck out of there and curl up in a ball on my bed at home. Unfortunately, there was no way out of the situation, as the throngs of people just grew and grew, and the rushes going through my head got stronger. Fuck me. I was out of my frigging head.

We had been standing in this queue for 30 minutes and didn't seem any closer to the entrance than when we'd first arrived. I was sweating big time and couldn't help but get fixated with the ear lobe of the geezer in front of me. It was amazing, but also a bit scary. I was sure it was pulsating. The ear hole then formed very subtle little lips around it and started trying to whisper something to me. Fuck that. I searched desperately for something else to look at. The fence that separated me from the rave proper suddenly took on a clarity and pattern and had an energetic rhythm that drew me to it. I was gripped by its glistening glory. I wanted to touch it. I wanted to feel it, but I couldn't reach it. There were too many little ear lobe creatures between me and its promised land.

There was a big surge and push from behind me. I stumbled a few metres forward and my face became wedged between the back and tits of two girls that were swaying to the music in the distance. I tried to pull my head out but couldn't. It was stuck. I just wanted to look at the magnificent, shimmering fence but was now looking into the depths of despair. I then heard my name.

"Wev? What the fuck are you doing?"

I tried looking up but was now obsessed with the cracks in the pavement. Where did they lead? Why were they moving? The soft tits of the girl on the right of me pushed my head against the hard back of the girl in front of me, with a force I hadn't experienced before. I heard my name again.

"Wev? Sort it out, mate."

The next vision I had was one of fire and smoke. It was bellowing in front of my eyes. Fuck, am I in the bowels of Hell? What was going on? I finally managed to prise my head free and breathed a deep breath of fresh air.

"Wev. I'm pleased you've finally managed to get your head out of my tits. Just take the fucking joint, will ya?"

It was Woo.

"What?"

"Sort yourself out, mate. You're fucked."

A sense of relief and elation overcame me.

"Thank fuck it's you. Have you seen all those weird ear-lobe people all over the place? They're doing my head in."

Woo and Letch just stood there laughing their asses off. I took a few deep drags on the joint and passed it ont o Letch. The marijuana added another layer of colour to my visuals, but at least it calmed my head down a bit. I grabbed Woo's arm and told her that I wasn't going to let go until we got inside. We were pushed and shoved for another 20 minutes until we finally reached the entrance to the rave. We were in. I was fucked and just didn't want to be there anymore. I was sweating profusely; there were too many people there. My sister and Letch dragged me to a stall that sold watermelon. They told me some liquid and a few vitamins should sort me out. I looked at the stall and freaked out. The watermelons looked like huge smiling red mouths. I spent the rest of the night sat on the floor trying my best not to look at, feel, or say anything. After an hour or so, my head sorted itself out, and I was able to join in with Woo and Letch on the ecstasy – but I've never looked at watermelon, or ear lobes, the same way ever again.

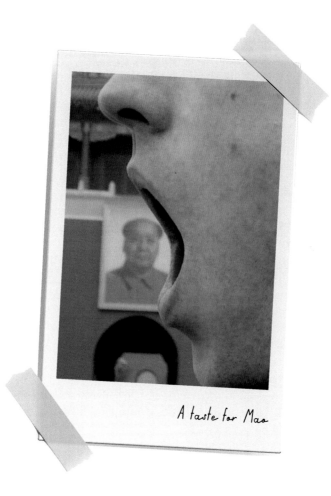

A taste for Mao

41.
HANGOVER CURE

I was slumped in a Xintiandi, Shanghai, restaurant, hungover, sitting opposite, La, a young lady whom I had picked up the night before. La had ordered a meal that she promised would make me feel a lot better. I was willing to try anything.

A waiter came over and plonked a glass bowl down on the table. It was full of grey, finger-sized prawns. Maybe 20 of them. They were still swimming. Alive.

"What the fuck is this?"

"Drunk prawn. Good for hangover."

The last thing I wanted was raw prawn for breakfast. Especially when my head was pounding. "Really?"

I looked back down at the bowl of prawns.

They looked back at me. They could – BECAUSE THEY WERE STILL ALIVE.

La looked at me and smiled an evil smile. "Yes. Good for hangover."

Next thing I knew, one of the prawns jumped out of the bowl and landed on the table. I jumped up in fright.

La laughed. "Hurry. Eat. Before prawn escape."

Not one to back down from doing something stupid, I took La's bait.

"Well, how do you eat these fuckers?"

She swept down on the prawn that had landed on the table and was now desperately trying to jump on to the floor and out the front door to the Huangpu River, and nimbly picked it up with her chopsticks. She stuck it in her mouth and bit it off at the head. The head was discarded of on the plate in front of her and a couple of seconds later, she gobbed the shell out on to the plate next to the guillotined head. She looked up at me expectantly. I looked at her and smiled. Now she had broken the live prawn seal, there was no stopping her, as she dived into the bowl of squirming and jumping prawns and picked another one up with her chopsticks and slammed it in her mouth, then again gobbed out the inedible bits on to her plate.

I looked at the prawn that was jumping and twerking it's batty at me on my plate, and picked it up with my chopsticks.

"Why you shake?" La said, pointing to my trembling hand.

I looked at the prawn. I felt sorry for it. And me.

Living in Hong Kong for four years had led me to be pretty nimble with chopsticks, but the cornucopia of cocktails I had imbibed the night before and the fact I was about to eat a live creature had led to my hands trembling uncontrollably. The prawn gave me a look of hatred from its weird peppercorn-like eyes, so I closed mine and stuffed its tail and body into my mouth and bit down just behind the head. The fishy juices of live prawn slithered down my throat. I bit at the base of the shell inside my mouth and sucked. The meat slid out of the shell and down my gullet. I then spat the shell on to my plate.

"It tastes of... booze," I said.

"Yes. Good for hangover, prawns swim in alcohol."

I polished off the bowl of pissed-up prawns and felt immediately tipsy and sick.

"Worst hair of the dog ever," I muttered grimly. And I should know – I've eaten an actual dog.

42.
THE BOMB

It was the 30 April 1999. Danger and I excitedly strutted down Dean Street, Soho, and crossed Old Compton Street to meet the lads outside the Scuzz House. We had been sitting in our coke dealer's office near Carnaby Street (yep – it was the nineties – he had an office) for too long, doing lines and smoking spliffs with him before we remembered we had a crew of people waiting for us at the Scuzz House, unable to properly start their night until some Peruvian was shovelled up their respective noses.

We then saw, and heard, a massive explosion.

Loud alarms. People screamed and yelled.

Most of the nearby windows of the shops and restaurants had smashed into smithereens, sending shards of glass on to the street. Then a steady stream of people started stumbling down the street with blood pouring from their heads, arms, and legs. There was just a mass of confusion.

What the fuck had just happened? Danger and I were petrified. We walked back to the corner of Old Compton Street and saw smoke and carnage coming out of the shell of what was the Admiral Duncan pub.

We had no idea what had happened, despite watching it happen in real time.

Danger and I wanted to run, but our feet wouldn't let us. Within minutes, the area was crawling with police and firemen. They began evacuating the area quickly.

With no idea what to do, Danger and I kept walking to the Scuzz House. When we arrived, all the lads had gone, but Michael, the owner, was still there.

"You guys need to leave," Michael said. "The police are evacuating the whole street."

What happened next, wasn't my proudest moment.

"Sure. But can we do a few lines before we leave," I said to Michael.

He rolled his eyes and said yes.

"We'll be quick, Michael. I promise."

Danger and I scurried down the stairs and racked up a couple of lines on the toilet seat. Just as I finished my second line, we heard some stomps down the stairs, and the toilet door open.

"Whoever is in there, get out now." This announcement was followed by some heavy, rapid knocking on the cubicle door.

"Er, hold on. I'll be out in a second," I shouted.

"You must leave now. We are evacuating the area."

It was the police.

"Fuck. OK. OK. I'm coming," I said. Danger and I just looked at each other in a panic. I whispered to Danger.

"How the fuck are we going to explain this?"

He just looked blankly at me. There was another impatient rap on the door.

"Come on. Get out."

I opened the door and was confronted by two scared-looking police officers. Their panicked look soon turned to a look of confusion, as Danger came out of the cubicle after me. They were clearly looking for survivors… and/or suspects? They didn't say a word. Knowing that my dilated pupils would be a big give away, I looked down at the floor as I tried to push past the policemen and out the toilet door. They didn't budge. I looked at the one who was blocking the doorway. They clearly knew what we had been doing.

"You are lucky we've got other shit to deal with tonight, otherwise you two would be in serious trouble," one of the officers said, wheezing.

With that, he stood aside and Danger and I scurried out of

the toilet and out on to the street, which looked like a war zone.

"Where shall we go now?" said Danger.

"Only one place to go," I said. "Carnaby Street."

Five minutes later, we were back upstairs in our dealer's offices, snorting more lines. Strangely, it felt the safest place in the city that night.

****

The next day, Danger and I found out that the explosion at the Admiral Duncan pub, one of Soho's most popular gay bars, had been a nailbomb. It had been detonated by some neo-Nazi lunatic who had set off similar bombs around London a few weeks prior to that night. Three people died and more than 70 were severely injured. It's a night I will never forget, despite my best efforts.

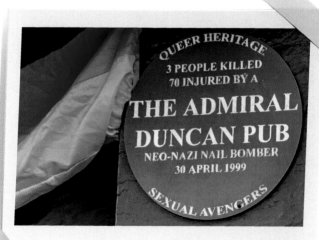

A bomb at the Admiral

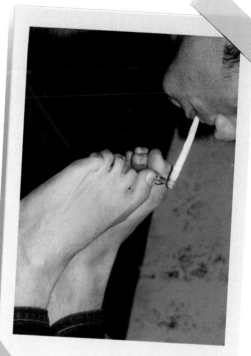

Smoke 'em if you got 'em

EPILOGUE

So, what did we learn? Firstly, a few things... *hopefully*. Secondly, I will never view myself as an author. I'm just an idiot who decided to write down all of the dope-ass shit that I have done throughout my life. All I hope is that it will inspire anyone who reads this to write, and more importantly, share the dumb shit that they've done. The world needs to celebrate stupidity – not be ashamed of it.

As I've written this book, I have gone to bed smiling every night. My mind just flowing with the various bits of nonsense that have made my life. Writing them down has really helped remember the detail and the funny moments that had been previously thrown in the area of your brain entitled "Forget". It's been great. I've literally had to catch myself from laughing out loud, whilst laying in bed on quite a few occasions. And who said that drugs don't work?

Catching up with mates I haven't spoken to in ages has also been a wonderful bonus that has come out of this whole process. Living abroad and having a family has meant that I had lost contact with most of the lads, but I am now in regular contact with each of them (apart from The Mule) and have regularly reminisced about our joint stupidity. It's been wonderful. We even set up a WhatsApp group where we keep in touch. Admittedly, the conversation has gone a bit stale now, as the initial conversations with each other quickly made us all realise why we stopped talking to begin with. So... what are all the cunts up to now?:

Kotch is teaching English, constantly obsessing over the culture wars, and enduring fatherhood (his words). He also still likes a mandolin medley, a light ale and Michael Flatley's *Riverdance* (my words).

Danger has been living in Cambodia for a number of years now. He still runs his company, but after comparing the women, rent and heroin of London's Soho and Phnom Penh, he felt he didn't really have much choice but to run his business from there. I've already put feelers out for a box-packing job with him, if things go hideously wrong this end.

Nelson has surprisingly not yet come out of the closet and is still a doting father and husband. He's still editing documentaries about Charlie Landsborough and others of his ilk and is living a nice little life in South London.

Fuck knows what The Mule is up to. Nelson sometimes pops out with him and has confirmed that he does still hate me. I reckon if he ever reads this book, he is gonna hate me even more, so I'm not expecting to rekindle any kind of friendship with the man. It's a shame, as we spent a good few years going through a lot of funny shit together. But there you have it.

Keels is back in the UK and has found himself a lovely wife who has spawned him a lovely child. He's given up on teaching and is now a diligent, highly-motivated and accomplished Programme / Project Manager with a proven track record of leading and delivering business improvements to secure operational excellence and value. Haha. He's about as diligent as my knob-end.

Chief is living the good life in some yard on the Laurie Lee Walk. He's got chickens, dogs and a whole heap of clutter that he turns into some other piece of clutter, that he turns into another piece of clutter that sometimes has a use. He's a well-known character on the festival circuit with his Chai Stall and Tibetan Café. He now looks very much like a Mongolian version of his mother.

Bon and his missus have decided to give up their lives in the theatre and in London, and move to a farm in Devon. They ain't gonna go totally feral on us, though, and are gonna use the land to rent yurts to unsuspecting urbanites, who will hopefully spend an extortionate amount of money for living in some accommodation that will look like something Chief has rustled up over the weekend.

MJ has been struck with long COVID, but is not getting all depressed about it. He's finally decided to take the plunge and get married to a very lucky young lady. He was a Grammar School Maths Teacher for seven years, then had a little injury, that turned into a big injury, and is now shuttling special needs kids to and from school.

As for me, in case you were wondering, I am still straight. I'm also still married. I still have two kids and I still have two cats. The pandemic didn't really affect me adversely. I managed to keep my job and earn a wage through the craziness that has happened. I've written a book and have even managed to enjoy a few trips away. Even my beloved West Ham have started winning more games than they are losing. So, all in all, I feel very blessed to still be "Wev". And while my hedonistic days of dope and danger are behind me, I still find the time to fill my days with stupidity. Some tigers never change their spots.

So, there you have it. Each and every one of us, have been absolute twats throughout our existence, but have turned out alright. In the end. *How the fuck did that happen?*

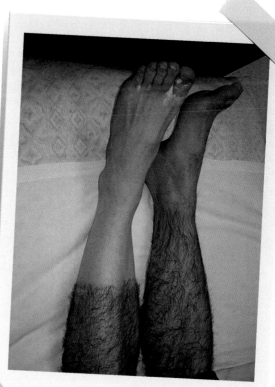

Still hasn't grown back

ACKNOWLEDGEMENTS

I need to split my thanks threefold:

1) The Professionals

Big Malc – what can I say, mon? You've turned my inane gibberings into something vaguely resembling a book. I can't thank you enough for the love, advice, inspiration and excellent work you have put into getting this shite into print. Tom – the design is fantastic. It looks far better than the content actually is, so fair play on that one. Da Pej – I can't thank you enough for sorting out the webshite.

2) The Motivators

The main man I need to thank here is my Dutch bredren, Greebo. He was the one that inspired me to write, as he was the one person that actually found my stories funny, when I would recite them over coffee. He then gave me the confidence that what I was writing was actually worthy of a book, so again, thanks, mon. This book wouldn't be in existence without you. Others to mention, are the other numptoids who put up with months of me sending them very rough first drafts of my stories on WhatsApp and the inspiration to keep on plugging away at this. In no particular order: Da Pej, TP, Danny Small, KT, Amine, De Impaler and Mutawa – nice one, gang.

3) My Fam and Friends

It must be near on impossible having to live with a fool like me, so I have nothing but gratitude and thanks for my friends and family for putting up with the constant ridicule, total lack of common sense and general Wevness they have all had to deal with over differing times in my life. Big love to all.

DOPEWEV.COM

ISBN 978-1-7397774-0-1

9 781739 777401 >